T0318702

Cambridge Elements ≡

Elements in Organization Theory
edited by
Nelson Phillips
Imperial College London
Royston Greenwood
University of Alberta

ORGANIZATIONAL LEARNING FROM PERFORMANCE FEEDBACK: A BEHAVIORAL PERSPECTIVE ON MULTIPLE GOALS

Pino G. Audia
Dartmouth College, New Hampshire

Henrich R. Greve
INSEAD, Singapore

CAMBRIDGE
UNIVERSITY PRESS

CAMBRIDGE
UNIVERSITY PRESS

University Printing House, Cambridge CB2 8BS, United Kingdom

One Liberty Plaza, 20th Floor, New York, NY 10006, USA

477 Williamstown Road, Port Melbourne, VIC 3207, Australia

314–321, 3rd Floor, Plot 3, Splendor Forum, Jasola District Centre, New Delhi – 110025, India

79 Anson Road, #06–04/06, Singapore 079906

Cambridge University Press is part of the University of Cambridge.

It furthers the University's mission by disseminating knowledge in the pursuit of education, learning, and research at the highest international levels of excellence.

www.cambridge.org
Information on this title: www.cambridge.org/9781108440936
DOI: 10.1017/9781108344289

First published 2021

A catalogue record for this publication is available from the British Library.

ISBN 978-1-108-44093-6 Paperback
ISSN 2397-947X (online)
ISSN 2514-3859 (print)

Organizational Learning from Performance Feedback: A Behavioral Perspective on Multiple Goals

Elements in Organization Theory

DOI: 10.1017/9781108344289
First published online: January 2021

Pino G. Audia
Dartmouth College, New Hampshire

Henrich R. Greve
INSEAD, Singapore

Author for correspondence: Pino G. Audia, Pino.G.Audia@tuck.dartmouth.edu

Abstract: This Element synthesizes the current state of research on organizational learning from performance feedback and develops a new perspective that deals with the influence of multiple goals. In keeping with the centrality of motives in Cyert and March's influential model, this new perspective rests on a foundation of individual-level behaviors that are responsive to mechanisms at the organizational and environmental level of analysis. A key aim is to lay out an agenda for a new wave of empirical research on the interconnections among decision-makers, organizations, and the environment that influence organizational responses to performance.

Keywords: Organizational learning, performance feedback, decision-making, organization theory, self-enhancement

ISBNs: 9781108440936 (PB), 9781108344289 (OC)
ISSNs: 2397-947X (online), 2514-3859 (print)

Contents

1 Introduction

This Element is about how organizations learn from performance feedback. The research it synthesizes and seeks to expand addresses issues of managerial and theoretical relevance that revolve around the origins of heterogeneity in organizational responses (and nonresponses) to performance that falls below an aspiration level. In other words, it deals with the question of when organizations respond to failure by making changes and when they don't. Although the original formulation of the theory specifies ways in which both individual decision-makers and organizations resolve the potential problem of goal conflict (Cyert and March, 1963), much of the empirical research on responsiveness to performance feedback is about single goals (for a recent review, see Posen, Keil, Kim, and Meissner, 2018). The relative inattention to multiple goals over the past twenty years is not a reflection of the original theory but rather an outcome of a very productive research stream that focused on a single goal – usually the return on assets (ROA). It is only recently that research has started to tackle the issue of how organizations respond to performance on multiple goals (Audia and Brion, 2007; Greve, 2008; Gaba and Joseph, 2013; Blagoeva et al., 2020). A key objective of this Element is to lay the foundation for a new wave of research on this important topic.

Before we explain why it is timely and advantageous to develop a multiple goals perspective on organizational learning from performance feedback, it is helpful to position this Element within the broader study of organizations. The theory of performance feedback is a key component of Cyert and March's (1963) "A Behavioral Theory of the Firm" – a groundbreaking book that was published at an early and formative stage of organizational theory, appearing as the third volume of the Carnegie School (Simon, 1947; March and Simon, 1958). The Carnegie School books (and articles) were influential because they constituted a break with two earlier forms of organizational theory (Hinings and Meyer, 2018). One earlier form originated in sociology and political science and sought to explain the rise of organizations in society and their broad characteristics (e.g., Blau, 1955; Weber, 1978). The other was composed of various texts seeking to extract principles of effective management (e.g., Barnard, 1938). The Carnegie School developed organizational theory that built on a strong micro foundation to take into account the bounded rationality of humans and its effect on structures and processes (Gavetti et al., 2012). Within the Carnegie School, Cyert and March (1963) were distinctive in their attention to organizational decision-making and their charge that economics had an incomplete theory of the firm because it ignored important processes that initiate and direct decision-making.

Currently, the theory of performance feedback is a branch of organizational learning, which is broadly defined as a "routine-based, history-dependent, and target-oriented" (Levitt and March, 1988: 319) activity that modifies organizational behaviors. A common thread in this extensive body of work lies in the importance it attributes to different forms of experience as antecedents of changes in cognitions and behaviors. Organizational learning is an essential research topic in the study of organizations because "learning capabilities are a basis for (the) strategic advantage" of firms (Levinthal and March, 1993: 23) and also because it is "inherently an interdisciplinary topic" (Argote and Miron-Spektor, 2011: 1123) that draws on and contributes to developments in organizational behavior and theory, sociology, economics, social psychology, and strategic management.

Within the study of organizational learning, the theory of performance feedback focuses on the target-oriented nature of the learning definition by holding that the performance on such targets – organizational goals – is a key influence on change. Research guided by this theory examines two ubiquitous and highly recurring organizational processes: How organizations assess whether performance is satisfactory and how these assessments impact decisions that result in organizational change. Although the theory was formulated more than fifty years ago (Cyert and March, 1963), organizational research on performance feedback continues to be highly influential as evidenced by a growing body of empirical work that supports and expands its key propositions.

Empirical work started by verifying some assumptions of the theory (Lant, 1992) and using it to examine changes in organizational risk taking (Singh, 1986; Bromiley, 1991) and change (Manns and March, 1978; Lant, Milliken, and Batra, 1992). The starting point of current research was a sequence of papers and a book that defined performance feedback as a driver of organizational change and examined some of its behavioral foundations (Greve, 1998, 2003a, 2003b, 2003c; Audia, Locke, and Smith, 2000). This simplified history omits important elements such as pioneering work on organizational change that was not followed up later (Manns and March, 1978), connections between the behavioral theory of the firm and other Carnegie School treatments (e.g., March and Simon, 1958), and a research tradition on firm risk taking (Fiegenbaum and Thomas, 1988; Fiegenbaum, 1990; Ruefli, 1990; Wiseman and Bromiley, 1991) using both the behavioral theory of the firm and theory on individual risk behaviors (Kahneman and Tversky, 1979). In the following sections, we do not dwell on history, but rather take stock of this theory in its current state and formulate theoretical developments meant to guide future research on what we see as important remaining topics.

To start, we propose a modified core model of performance feedback that builds on Cyert and March's (1963) and Greve's (2003c) previous representations in two important ways. First, it integrates the view that performance is assessed in relation not only to an aspiration level but also to a survival point (March and Shapira, 1992; Audia and Greve, 2006). Second, it relaxes the assumption that decision-makers' sole motivation is to address problems flagged by low performance (problem-solving orientation) by adding that they may be also motivated to maintain a positive image (self-enhancement orientation; Audia and Brion, 2007; Jordan and Audia, 2012). These modifications help provide behavioral accounts for the long-standing puzzle of organizations that do not change in response to low performance as much as neutral observers would expect. Drawing on a growing body of empirical work, the modified core model specifies conditions that prompt shifts of attention across reference points (i.e., aspiration levels and the survival point) and switches between problem-solving and self-enhancement modes.

Next, we draw on the theoretical advances incorporated in the modified core model of performance feedback to revisit and expand the neglected component of the theory that deals with the influence of multiple goals. The timing for giving greater attention to multiple goals is favorable for two reasons – one internal to the theory of performance feedback and the other stemming from developments in organization theory. First, theoretical advances made over the past fifteen years have expanded the theoretical foundation of the theory in ways that enable a better understanding of how decision-makers respond to multiple goals. We are thinking especially about the now well-developed idea of shifts of attention across reference points and across goals as well as the resurging interest in the influence of the hierarchy on responses to multiple goals (March and Shapira, 1992; Greve, 2008; Gaba and Joseph, 2013; Kacperczyk, Beckman, and Moliterno, 2015). These developments internal to the theory imply important differences in the way responses to performance on multiple goals occur at different levels of the organization.

Second, several influential strands of organization theory converge in noting that organizations now more than ever are pressured by external influences to pursue goals that are hard to achieve simultaneously. Goals are added to satisfy the demands of environments characterized by "multiple logics," "conflicting logics," "institutional complexity," or "the blurring between sectoral boundaries" (Thornton, 2002; Battilana and Dorado, 2010; Greenwood et al., 2011). As Bromley and Meyer (2015: 141) note, "firms pursue corporate responsibility, nonprofits adopt risk management practices, and government agencies implement performance measurement." Clearly, organizations today are facing a new set of challenges surrounding the pursuit of goals. Renewed attention to multiple goals in research on performance feedback helps lay a theoretical foundation for a deeper understanding of the individual- and meso-level mechanisms that account for organizational action in response to these complex environments. We advance a view in which conditions such as the relative salience of different motives among managers, the degree of centralization and formalization of the organizational structure, the amount of power possessed by managers, and environmental features such as the degree of institutional complexity and formalization influence responsiveness to performance on multiple goals.

In keeping with the strong microfoundation that characterizes theories associated to the Carnegie School (Gavetti et al. 2012), we formalize these considerations in an extended model of performance feedback that rests on a foundation of individual-level behaviors but is responsive to mechanisms at the organizational and environmental level of analysis. By developing the model in this order, we take advantage of component theories at each level of analysis that did not exist when the behavioral theory of the firm was formulated (Cyert and March, 1963). Our objective is to lay foundations for more empirical research on the interconnections of decision-makers, organizations, and the environment that influence organizational responses to performance.

We view the extended theory of performance feedback we outline as an attempt to strengthen the components of the theory regarding agency and the influence of the context. The greater emphasis on multiple goals amplifies the theoretical and empirical challenge of determining how organizations and their managers respond to heterogeneous feedback that can be plausibly interpreted in different ways. Agency results from shifts in attention across performance goals, variations in assessments of success and failure, and consequent behaviors. The context also plays a greater role, whether it is the internal context of the organization or the external context of the environment, because it creates conditions that influence the activation of motives that guide responsiveness to goals and because it proposes goals as solutions to managers oriented toward fulfilling varying motives.

We begin with a discussion of main concepts and theoretical mechanisms, both those used in most or all current treatments and those that have been specified but still not been used much. This treatment is not meant to be a complete overview, because it is targeted toward putting in place the theoretical components that are most needed for advancing research on performance and aspiration effects on organizational change.

Because research on performance and aspirations is so active currently, there are also other treatments with goals complementary to this Element. Some examine empirical research on goals and aspirations (Shinkle, 2012;

Kotiloglu, Chen, and Lechler, 2019) and search (Posen et al., 2018), whereas others propose theoretical cross-fertilization with institutional theory (Greve and Teh, 2018) and group-level research (Greve and Gaba, 2020). Because our goal is to identify the main areas that need theoretical development and empirical investigation, we selectively draw from this work as we develop our argument.

2 The Core Model of Performance Feedback: Goals, Aspiration Levels, Search, and Change

In the behavioral theory of the firm, organizational action is driven by goals, which are defined as important outcomes and are usually assigned to the entire organization or a subunit of the organization (Cyert and March, 1963). The organization regularly gathers information on the performance on each goal and evaluates it. Organizational members classify performance as satisfactory or unsatisfactory using an acceptable-level decision rule. Performance over a certain level is acceptable and indicates that no change is needed, but performance below means that the organization has a problem that it addresses by intensifying the search for new solutions and the introduction of change. This acceptable level, which is a minimally acceptable performance, is referred to as the aspiration level.[1]

The process of classifying performance into satisfactory and unsatisfactory is quite important because it reveals that it is not performance per se that influences behavior but rather how performance is assessed. In the original formulation of the theory, the aspiration level is the key standard against which performance is assessed and it is derived from two distinct sources of information: own past performance, which can be used to form a historical aspiration level, and peers' performance, which can be used to form a social aspiration level. Own past performance is arguably the closest approximation to a natural standard for classifying future performance into satisfactory and unsatisfactory. Information about how well an individual, an organizational function, or an entire organization did in the past is easily available and tends to be highly salient. It also yields evaluations that are easily understood: Increases in performance over time are generally regarded positively because they are viewed as a sign that improvements were made. Conversely, declines in performance over time are generally viewed as evidence of deficiencies that need attention. The ease with which we resort to comparisons of current and past performance may be a reason why we don't need any justification when we hear reports of companies' financial results in the form of percentage variations in relation to

---

[1] This is different from the colloquial meaning of "aspiration" as a goal to strive for.

past performance. Using past performance as a natural standard for the assessment of performance seems to be a taken-for-granted practice.

Performance may be classified into satisfactory or unsatisfactory also by using the performance of peers as a standard of evaluation. Festinger's (1954: p. 117) example of a person who assesses whether he is a slow or a fast runner by comparing his performance to the performance of people in the same age group is a case in point. Similarly, it is easy to envision how managers find it meaningful to determine whether their organizations achieve satisfactory or unsatisfactory performance by simply comparing their organizational performance to the performance of peer organizations. What sets peers' performance apart from own past performance as an information source is that in some situations information about peers is not easily available. When this constraint is absent, however, a social aspiration, just like a historical aspiration, enables boundedly rational managers to assess performance in an efficient yet credible fashion.

The core model of performance feedback has become such an integral part of organizational theory that it is easy to overlook its appeal. First, the acceptable-level decision rule means that organizations are oriented less toward opportunities than toward problem-solving. This is different from rational choice and a broad family of theories that see organizations as opportunity-seeking. It also means that the intensity of problem-solving may be less a smooth function of the performance level than a discontinuous result of falling below the acceptable level. The formation of an aspiration level means that problems are defined by other conditions than the current state of the organization because it is based either on previous performance (historical) or on the performance of other organizations (social). It also means that the aspiration level adapts over time, though again in ways that reflect other features than the organizational opportunities. Also, orienting search toward solving specific problems means that interdependencies between performance measures and the responsible units of the organization can easily be overlooked. Search for solutions can be done in the proximity of the problem, but it can also be done elsewhere in the organization (Cyert and March, 1963: 121–122). As a final step, search is concluded when a solution is found that has an expected outcome better than the aspiration level. Failure to find such solutions or disappointing performance after implementing them can start search again and expand the scope of the search. In combination, the decision-making steps in this model suggest a much less rational and optimizing view of organizations than is commonly assumed.

In Table 1, the first panel summarizes the main concepts introduced by Cyert and March (1963) and used in research on performance feedback. The table also looks forward to the developments that follow. In the next section, we integrate

Table 1 The evolution of performance feedback models

Core Model (Cyert and March, 1963)
Goals are what the organization seeks to accomplish
Performance is the level of accomplishment on a goal
Aspiration level is the performance level that separates satisfying and non-satisfying outcomes
A problem-solving orientation motivates decision-makers to seek to solve the problem of performance below the aspiration level through so-called problemistic search
Change happens when an alternative that seems to solve the problem has been found
Modified Core Model (1992–2020)
Kinked-curve relation means lesser responsiveness to performance below aspiration level (Greve, 1998)
Survival point is the performance level below which disastrous outcomes occur (March and Shapira, 1992; Audia and Greve, 2006)
A self-enhancement orientation motivates decision-makers to assess performance in favorable ways (Audia and Brion, 2007)
Shift of attention from the aspiration level to the survival point and self-enhancing responses to low performance account for the kinked-curve relation
Extended Model (2020)
A problem-solving response means that decision-makers direct attention to goals that show low performance and initiate search and change
A self-enhancing response means that decision-makers direct attention to goals that show high performance and do not initiate search and change
High individual involvement, high ambiguity, and high individual power increase self-enhancing and reduce problem-solving responses to performance on multiple goals
High organizational centralization, high formalization, and low subunit power increase problem-solving and reduce self-enhancing responses to performance on multiple goals
High institutional complexity, low environmental formalization, and high organizational power increase self-enhancing and reduce problem-solving responses to performance on multiple goals

findings from research conducted since Greve's (2003c) book to propose a modified core model of performance feedback. The theoretical advances that result in this modified core model stem from studies that sought to account for what is known in this body of work as the kinked-curve performance-change relation (Greve, 1998). Table 1 summarizes the three concepts central to this theoretical development and current empirical work on performance feedback. In this Element, we also look forward and specify an extended model that is motivated in part not only by recent work on organizations with multiple goals but also by evidence on single-goal performance feedback that does not fully fit the modified core model. This extended model is developed in Section 5. This also summarizes its main additions to the theory.

3 The Modified Core Model

The core model of performance feedback draws significantly from Cyert and March (1963) and can be viewed as a research stream relying on the same theoretical foundation but using a modernized empirical approach. As this research stream developed, however, theoretical modifications were also made, leading to the modified core model. The kinked-curve relation, the survival point, and self-enhancement were the central new theoretical mechanisms added. Figure 1 illustrates how these mechanisms were implemented empirically, providing a summary of the core model and the modifications to it.

As Figure 1 shows, the core model is a simple linear progression from performance below the aspiration level through problemistic search to organizational change. The actual empirical models had more detail because they recognized that search and change could also happen above the aspiration level. The theory had another layer of detail because it specified how the aspiration level was formed and how search was conducted. The modified core model added the kinked-curve relation, the survival point, and self-enhancement. Again, the figure shows how these were implemented empirically as factors modifying the relation to the rate of change. The theory had additional detail. For example, the kinked-curve relation moved away from the original linear

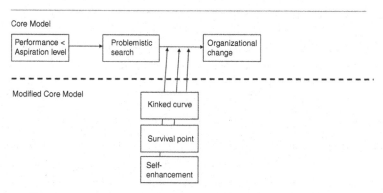

Figure 1 Core and modified core model of performance feedback

relation from performance to change to suggest the importance of treating performance above and below the aspiration level as distinct antecedents of change. Subsequently, we develop these details to show the current state of the modified core model.

3.1 The Conundrum of the Kinked-Curve Relation

Early formulations of the theory did not specify the functional form of the relationship between performance in relation to an aspiration level and the propensity to search and make changes. This left open the possibility that changes in performance over the entire range of performance would have the same effect on these organizational behaviors (e.g., Lant, Milliken, and Batra, 1992; Miller and Chen, 1994). Greve (1998), in an influential study, suggested that responses to performance in relation to an aspiration level differ depending on whether performance is above or below an aspiration level. Specifically, he proposed that the impetus for change stemming from unsatisfactory performance is fraught with more resistance than the commitment to the status quo arising from satisfactory performance. Unsatisfactory performance plants the seed for motivating the search for new solutions and change, but the extent to which these behaviors materialize hinges on the strength of other processes that underlie resistance to change. Greve found initial evidence of this discontinuity or kink in the slope of the relationship between performance in relation to an aspiration level and change in a study of radio stations. Audience share below the aspiration level increased the probability of the introduction of new radio formats less strongly than audience share above it decreased it, producing a kinked-curve relation from audience share to format change. Later empirical work found additional evidence of change behaviors being less sensitive to performance below an aspiration level than above it. A study of shipbuilders found that performance above an aspiration level decreased the propensity to launch innovations, whereas performance below an aspiration level did not have any effect (Greve, 2003a). Likewise, a study of hard disk drive producers found that the propensity to introduce new hard disk drives was negatively impacted by performance above an aspiration level but it was not significantly affected by performance below an aspiration level (Audia and Brion, 2007: Study 2). Works such as Baum and Dahlin's study of railroad firms (2007) and Diwas, Staats, and Gino's study of cardiac surgery (2013) lend additional support by reporting that both organizations and individuals learn more from high performance than from low performance.

The fact that organizations initiate searches for new solutions or make changes less readily in response to performance below an aspiration level than previously assumed poses a theoretical conundrum that current formulations of the theory resolve by suggesting that managers' attention is not necessarily fixed at all times on an aspiration level. Attention shifts between different standards of evaluations and these shifts yield variations in responses to unsatisfactory performance. The theoretical question then becomes: What mechanisms can account for these shifts of attention?

3.2 Responsiveness to Performance and the Survival Point

The first account draws on March and Shapira's (1992) shifting focus model of risk-taking, which introduces the notion of a survival point as an alternative standard of evaluation. March and Shapira propose conditions under which managers shift their standard of evaluation from an aspiration level to a survival point defined as the point at which all resources are depleted and the organization fails. Drawing on theories of threat rigidity (Staw, Sandelands, and Dutton, 1981) and risk (Lopes, 1987), they suggest that when such a shift occurs managers become risk-averse. The rationale is that attention to a survival point implies a heightened concern for security that deters managers from taking actions that have uncertain outcomes and thus may lead to catastrophic outcomes.

March and Shapira's (1992) analysis is not strictly about how performance is assessed but rather about how managers assess an organization's stock of resources. Indeed, its theoretical connection to the study of responsiveness to performance feedback was made more than ten years after its publication. Drawing on March and Shapira's shifting focus model, Audia and Greve (2006) suggest that whether managers focus their attention on an aspiration level or on a survival point depends on which of the two is closer to actual performance. In their analysis, attention goes to the standard closest to performance because the consequences of reaching the closer point loom larger. So, when low performance is closer to the survival point, the concern for avoiding a catastrophic outcome outweighs the desire to improve performance. Low performance is seen as a step closer to failure rather than as a repairable gap. Fear and the need for safety prevail over the desire to improve (Lopes, 1987). Audia and Greve view an organization's stock of resources as a key influence on the position of a survival point, both cognitively and in reality, because resources such as financial assets, manufacturing infrastructures, and a large workforce allow organizations to endure many periods of poor financial performance with little threat of failure (Levinthal, 1991). This buffering effect of a large stock of resources lowers the performance level at which the organization's survival is in danger, in essence rendering a survival point more distant and less salient. Small resource endowments, in contrast, raise the level of an organization's survival point and thus heighten awareness of the distance between performance and the survival point.

Taking an organization's size as a proxy for the stock of resources, they suggest that managers of small and large firms will respond differently to performance below an aspiration level. When compared to managers of large firms, small firms perceive that performance below an aspiration is closer to the survival point. These perceptions should prompt a greater concern for security and a diminished propensity to take actions with uncertain outcomes such as those involving the search for new solutions and the introduction of change. Given these heterogeneous responses, what may appear in aggregate reduced organizational responsiveness to low performance or insensitivity to low performance may mask variations in responsiveness of small and large organizations.

Audia and Greve's (2006) empirical analyses of the factory expansion of shipbuilders support this argument. Large shipbuilders generally invest in factory expansion less than small shipbuilders, a finding consistent with the idea that bureaucratic constraints make large firms inert and risk-averse, but large shipbuilders increase factory expansion more than small shipbuilders in response to performance below an aspiration level. Greve (2011) replicates these results in a sample of shipping firms. In response to low performance, large shipping firms, compared to small firms, acquire more ships as well as ships more different from the ones they already have. Both studies also reveal decreased propensities to make changes when performance is above an aspiration level. Whereas these studies focus on size as a proxy of the stock resources, later empirical work extends this reasoning to other resources that may serve as buffers from threats to the survival of the organization. Desai (2008) examines positive media coverage as a proxy for legitimacy in a study of capacity expansion of railroad firms, whereas Lehman et al. (2011) focus on deadline proximity as an indicator of time scarcity in a study of fourth-down decisions made by football teams. In both instances, the findings are supportive of variations in responsiveness to low performance as a function of resources that buffer from catastrophic outcomes: A smaller stock of resources is associated with a more muted response to low performance, in line with empirical evidence of a kink in the slope of the relationship between performance in relation to an aspiration level and the propensity to make changes.

3.3 Self-enhancing Assessments of Low Performance

A second account of organizations' lesser responsiveness to low performance comes from research that draws on the social psychological literature on self-enhancement, people's desire to view the self, and to have others view the self, in the most positive light possible (Kunda, 1990; Sedikides and Strube, 1997; Pfeffer and Fong, 2005). A key contingency in this work is the ambiguity that is often encountered when assessing performance (Audia and Brion, 2007).

Research on self-enhancement holds that feedback that is ambiguous, meaning that it is open to multiple interpretations, is often interpreted in favorable ways because favorable interpretations of performance enable individuals to maintain a positive image (Dunning et al., 1989). The inclination to tackle performance deficits by searching for new solutions and making changes is still important but it is especially relevant when performance is unambiguously unsatisfactory (Jordan and Audia, 2012; Audia, Brion, and Greve, 2015). In unambiguous situations, self-serving assessments of low performance would be difficult to defend because evaluative assessments reflect not only what people want to believe but also what dispassionate observers consider credible (Kunda, 1990).

Ambiguity surrounding performance assessment may arise in different ways. Much of the empirical research reviewed earlier focuses on a single perform-ance measure but when other performance measures are taken into account ambiguity may arise as a result of performance measures that give different signals. Audia and Brion (2007) examine how individuals and organizations respond to situation in which a secondary performance measure diverges from a primary performance measure. Consideration of two performance measures that vary in importance is particularly revealing because, if the desire to be accurate guides behavior, a primary performance measure should hold more weight in guiding behavior than a secondary performance measure. This implies that, when performance on a primary performance measure is low, it should not make any difference whether a secondary performance measure is above or below an aspiration level. Audia and Brion find, however, that a primary performance measure that falls below an aspiration level instigates less change when a secondary performance measure is above an aspiration level than when a secondary performance measure is also below an aspiration level. In addition, they find that when a secondary performance measure is more favorable than a primary performance measure, individuals rearrange the hierarchy of the two performance measures giving more importance to the secondary performance measure. Audia and Brion (2007) find supporting evidence of self-enhancing interpretations of diverging performance measures and lower responsiveness to performance below an aspiration level both in an experimental study of indi-vidual decision-makers (Study 1) and in an archival study of disk drive produ-cers (Study 2). Blagoeva, Mom, Jansen, and George (2020) report additional evidence of self-enhancing responses to performance on multiple goals in a study of R&D investments.

Ambiguity may also result from performance comparisons to multiple aspir-ation levels. Joseph and Gaba (2015) study divergences in aspirations over time in the global mobile phone industry. They argue that managers take into account how market share changes over time in relation to both historical and social aspiration levels and respond differently to feedback that is consistent (positively correlated), inconsistent (negatively correlated), and ambiguous (weakly linked). Consistent feedback sends an unequivocal signal of either improvement or decline and should trigger decreases or increases in the propensity to make change, respectively, in line with the predictions of the theory. Inconsistent feedback is also easy to interpret, they propose, because it is difficult to paint rosy pictures of situations in which organizations are improving over their past performance but at a slower rate than that of their competitors or when they are doing better than their competitors but worse off than their past performance. In both instances, they predict that inconsistent feedback increases change. Ambiguous feedback, evidenced by performance patterns that are neither distinctly improving nor declining, creates greater opportunities for favorable interpretations. Under conditions of ambiguity, managers perceive that they can form defensible favorable assessments by, for example, giving greater weight to information that is positive and casting doubt on information that is negative. Because of these favorable interpretations, Joseph and Gaba suggest that ambiguous feedback should reduce responsiveness to performance. Their empirical analyses of global mobile phone firms' propensity to introduce new products in response to their market share support these predictions. Lucas, Knoben, and Meeus (2018) find a similar pattern of self-enhancing responses to performance feedback when diverging aspirations introduce ambiguity in performance assessment. Audia, Brion, and Greve (2015) lend additional support to self-enhancing responses to low performance by showing in an experimental setting that, when performance is low, decision-makers select social comparisons that are favorable. Smith and Chae (2017) extend their finding showing how self-enhancing selections of favorable social comparisons are enabled by the ambiguity of organizational forms.

3.4 Integrating Survival Point and Self-enhancement Accounts of the Kinked Curve

To summarize, two key observations emerge from this body of work. First, there is considerable evidence supporting the view that responses to performance in relation to an aspiration level differ depending on whether performance is above or below an aspiration level. Specifically, the impetus for change stemming from unsatisfactory performance is fraught with more resistance than the commitment to the status quo arising from satisfactory performance (Greve, 1998). Unsatisfactory performance plants the seed for motivating the search for new solutions and change but the extent to which these behaviors materialize hinges on the strength of other processes that underlie resistance to change. Second, two distinct mechanisms contribute to accounting for the kink in the relationship. The first mechanism concerns switches of attention away from an aspiration to a survival point that are likely to occur when performance is low, and organizations have a limited stock of resources. These shifts of attention are concomitant to a heightened concern for safety that deters managers from taking actions that have uncertain outcomes and thus can cause the organization to fail. The second mechanism concerns self-enhancing interpretations of low performance rendered possible by ambiguity arising from diverging performance measures or from weakly linked performance assessments stemming from multiple aspiration levels. In these instances, ambiguity enables managers, who are generally inclined to portray negative outcomes in a favorable way, to formulate defensible self-serving assessments.

The prevalent approach in recent empirical work has been to identify contextual features such as an organization's stock of resources and sources of ambiguity in performance assessment that heighten the influence of, respectively, a survival point or self-serving assessments of performance. Research addressing conditions that activate these mechanisms has proceeded separately but there are interdependencies that require consideration. Both self-enhancement and attention to the survival point predict decreased responsiveness to low performance but the theory suggests different conditions triggering these two distinct mechanisms. Self-enhancement is enabled by ambiguity (Audia and Brion, 2007; Joseph and Gaba, 2015). When ambiguity is low, self-enhancing interpretations are less likely and the problem-solving mode is likely to guide action. Under conditions of low ambiguity, when room for favorable interpretations of low performance is lacking, low performance may trigger a focus of attention on the survival point when decision-makers perceive a threat to vital interests (Audia and Greve, 2006). This is likely to happen when the stock of resources is depleted to a point that additional instances of unequivocal low performance create a precarious state for the organization and/or the members responsible for the performance. Under those conditions, resources that buffer from safety concerns are expected to impact attention to the survival point. The stock of tangible assets creates differences in perceptions of safety among small and large firms that are equally low performing. Similarly, the degree of support from external stakeholders accounts for variations in perceptions that safety is at risk when performance is low (Desai, 2008) and sport teams feel closer to the survival point when time is running out during a match (Lehman et al., 2011). So to infer whether low responsiveness to low performance stems from self-enhancing assessments or from attention to the survival point, the modified core model suggests considering the degree of ambiguity confronted by decision-makers who assess performance and the stock of resources indicative of proximity to the survival point.

Two types of studies are particularly valuable as researchers seek to identify when self-enhancement or attention to the survival point prevail in influencing responses to low performance. Longitudinal studies of organizations (e.g., Greve, 2008) and individuals (e.g., Audia and Goncalo, 2007) in which attention to different standards of evaluation is not directly examined but is inferred from the kind of responses to performance researchers observe in the data will continue to be a valuable source of insights. These studies can identify and test the influence of characteristics of the organizations and the environments that are theoretically linked to distinct mechanisms. The modified core model, with its greater emphasis on variations in the process of performance assessment, also calls for research that directly examines how organizations form standards of evaluation and how they direct their attention to them (e.g., Audia, Brion, and Greve, 2015; Smith and Chae, 2017). This research can include examination of organizations with goals that are distinct because they are not conventional firms but rather hybrid organizations, voluntary organizations, or governmental organizations.

Research on goal and aspiration level formation is a direction that was pursued early on by researchers interested in performance feedback (e.g., Lant, 1992) and that has started to gain renewed interest. The research has addressed a wide range of questions. First, there are alternative models of aspiration level updating, all of which originate from Cyert and March but make some modifications such as entering an upward drift or separating the historical and social aspiration level. Because the first studies were experimental, later work added investigations of aspiration level updating using data from firms (Mezias, Chen, and Murphy, 2002). Other work has tested different aspiration level specifications for fit against broad databases of firms (Bromiley and Harris, 2014). Still other work investigates aspiration levels that combine social awareness and historical performance in new ways (Moliterno et al., 2014), identifies specific effects of social and historical performance comparisons (Kacperczyk et al., 2015), or captures interorganizational differences in aspiration level updating (Blettner et al., 2015). The findings have not fundamentally altered how aspiration levels are modeled, but they have pointed to ways in which empirical measurement and theory can be improved.

The modifications of the core model of performance feedback are important for at least two reasons. The first is that they provide theoretically driven and empirically supported accounts of the long-standing puzzle of why organizations often fail to learn from failure. Clearly, the extent to which a theory of performance feedback offers persuasive and testable explanations of organizations' lack of responsiveness to low performance is a key indication of its strength. The second is that they integrate into the model of performance assessment originally developed by Cyert and March well developed concepts

such as the survival point and self-enhancing interpretations of low performance that offer additional opportunities for expanding the predictive power of
the model. An important by-product of the work that tackles the conundrum of
the kinked curve is that it brings renewed attention to multiple goals. Indeed,
according to the modified core model, muted responses to low performance are
often due to shifts of attention across goals. These shifts of attention were an
important insight in the original version of the theory. Next, we turn our
attention to the component of the theory regarding the influence of multiple
goals on search and change and discuss theoretical advances that expand on
these original insights. We will find that research on multiple goals, although
still in its infancy, has already made enough advances to suggest opportunities
to create an extended model of performance feedback and provide guidance on
what its components should be.

4 Multiple Goals

A defining feature of any organization is the set of goals it pursues. The goals
organizations set, monitor, and report on are highly varied. Some – such as
return on assets or a corporate social responsibility index – capture the overall
contribution organizations make to distinct stakeholders. Others – such as sales,
innovation, safety, or business unit revenue – identify the contribution that
distinct subunits make to the overall outcomes of the organization.
Organizations *have* goals and *use* goals. They have goals set by founders and
stakeholders, and these are associated with the economic role and social identity
of the organization. They are the types of goals that specify that a commercial
bank is a profit-seeking organization that provides financial services including
loans and deposits. A thrift bank or a commercial bank with a community
orientation will have variations of these goals. Organizations use goals to direct
decision-making and motivate employees, and these are usually designed to
"add up" to the overall organizational goals. Under bounded rationality, there is
no guarantee that they do so. Consequently, the goals that organizations use may
be in conflict with the goals they have. The goals organizations use are more
specialized and include those that might specify details such as the desired year-
on-year sales increase by a mortgage loans officer.

For developing a more differentiated and realistic theory, the key point is that
"organizations develop multiple goals and sub-goals ... on several dimensions
reflecting inconsistent and manifold arenas" (Bromley and Meyer, 2015). The
goal structure of organizations is in part a result of how goals map on to the
organizational structure, but there are added complications such as the tension
between subunit goals and the organizational goals when the two suggest different decisions and the tension of goals within individuals and among individuals

who participate in team decision-making. For example, consider the mortgage officer processing a potential loan that is flagged as too risky by the risk assessment software. This officer may have a subunit goal to lend more, have a personal career goal of fast promotion, have an intuition that this lender is less risky than the software assessment indicates, and may know how to manipulate the numbers to reclassify the mortgage as less risky. Which goal will the loan officer focus on? It would be too much to ask for a precise prediction, but the general theory should be able to incorporate such specific concerns.

4.1 Vertical Differentiation of Goals

Organizations are hierarchical systems that coordinate behaviors at different levels, learn at different levels, and have goals at different levels. The structure of goals within organizations was an important topic in early work (March and Simon, 1958), with a focus on how high-level goals could be decomposed to sub-goals at lower levels that let boundedly rational decision-makers reach a nearly optimal set of behaviors from the organizational point of view. This differentiation of goals was less prominent in the behavioral theory of the firm, which had less of a focus on organizational design and more on organizational behavior (Cyert and March, 1963). Research is returning to this issue now that the observation of goals at different levels has spurred interest in how they interrelate.

Vertical differentiation of goals has also been a topic of recent research, but without the goal composition element of the early work. Instead, goals at different levels have been seen as potentially reinforcing and potentially rivaling. This research is built on observations such as the presence of the same goal (ROA) at both corporate and division levels (Gaba and Joseph, 2013), as well as profitability goals at higher levels interacting with other goals at lower levels (Audia and Sorenson, 2001; Joseph, Klingebiel, and Wilson, 2016). The findings suggest a clear tension between the relevance of a lower-level goal and the hierarchical (and survival-related) priority of higher-level profitability. At its current stage, however, this research is more an invitation to further theory development than a conclusive statement. Because the higher-level goal in the studies so far has been ROA, which is known for its great behavioral impact regardless of organizational level, it is unclear whether its effect strength reflects the high hierarchical position or the nature of the goal.

4.2 Horizontal Differentiation of Goals

Intraorganizational goals are also horizontally differentiated, and again this can be seen as a consequence of overall goals being decomposed. Indeed, the listing of sales, inventory, and production goals by Cyert and March (1963: 117) suggests exactly such a decomposition toward the main goal of profitability. Organizations deal with the dilemma that each goal is associated with one (or more) organizational units, however, and often have structures that do not encourage and facilitate coordination among the multiple decomposed goals. It still seems obvious that coordination occurs at some level, as the juxtaposition of these three goals suggests, but this leaves open the question of how the organization responds to falling behind on any of these goals, either as a stated aspiration level or one with a historical or social source. Research on horizontally differentiated goals is completely absent as far as we have been able to determine, as the focus has been on comparisons of vertically differentiated goals. This is probably because vertically differentiated goals are a more salient feature of the empirical reality of interest to management scholars, but the low interest in horizontally differentiated goals is still a striking omission.

4.3 Externally Imposed Goals

The single most important advance in organizational theory since Cyert and March's (1963) behavioral theory of the firm has been the increased focus on the organizational environment as an influence on organizational behaviors (Scott, 1987). Interestingly, work on how performance and aspiration levels affect organizational behaviors has been late to incorporate these insights and has instead followed the original focus on internal organizational goals. However, there is increased realization that organizations also face externally imposed goals, starting with the observation that institutions often impose rule-like compliance and monitoring by external actors (Meyer and Rowan, 1977) and continuing to the recent attention to the effects of external rating and ranking systems on organizations (Sauder and Espeland, 2009). Although empirical examination of the effects of external goals is limited, recognition of these effects has led external actors to use public rankings to change organizational behaviors (Bartley and Child, 2011). Initial evidence suggests that such interventions have some success (Chatterji and Toffel, 2010; Sharkey and Bromley, 2015; Rowley, Shipilov, and Greve, 2017; Shipilov, Greve, and Rowley, 2019).

4.4 Behavioral Consequences of Multiple Goals

Cyert and March (1963) proposed two solutions to a scenario in which organizational members react to performance on multiple goals. The first is sequential attention to goals. Because they do not have the cognitive capacity to simultaneously attend to multiple goals, managers cope with their bounded rationality by tackling goals sequentially. They start by tackling the goal highest in a hierarchy of importance. When the performance on that goal is satisfactory, they move their attention and effort toward the pursuit of the next goal in the hierarchy. Underlying the idea of sequential attention to goals are the assumptions that a goal hierarchy exists and that managers display consistency in adhering to this goal hierarchy.

The second solution to the multiplicity of goals sheds light on how a goal hierarchy emerges. Cyert and March (1963) suggest that groups inside organizations have conflicting interests that are often reflected in the importance they assign to different goals. Through a process of negotiation and power accumulation, a dominant coalition emerges that temporarily shapes goal priorities. So, when more than one goal can be plausibly seen as most critical for the organization, the dominant coalition addresses the potential goal conflict by giving greater weight to the goal that aligns with the views of its members. That goal becomes the primary concern even if other groups within the organization may have different preferences. Importantly, Cyert and March (1963) highlight the unstable nature of this internal equilibrium, noting that it involves continuing negotiation and that it depends on side payments of resources in return for support from groups. In essence, goal conflict is often unresolved and inconsistency among goals complicates understanding of how organizations respond to multiple goals.

Current theory has moved beyond these core ideas regarding multiple goals. New insights have emerged at different levels of analyses. Because the majority of the empirical work on learning from performance feedback focused on responsiveness to performance on a single goal, multiple goals were initially brought in to address the puzzle of the kinked curve and more generally of muted responses to low performance. Later research examined multiple goals because they are such a well-known feature of organizational life, but we believe that their theoretical implications have not yet been developed fully. In this Element we propose that multiple goals should become more prominent in the study of responsiveness to performance feedback. Taking this perspective, instead of assuming the primacy of a single goal, researchers would start by considering multiple goals that are important to organizations and their subunits and seek to explain why and when decision-makers across the organizational hierarchy respond to performance on a particular goal. Such a theoretical and empirical move would help develop a deeper understanding of how features of the organizational context and the external environment alter attention and responsiveness to goals. In Section 5, we develop an extended model of performance feedback building on theory at the individual level of analysis, but also taking into consideration influences at the organizational and environmental levels of analysis. The purpose is to outline promising areas of research and theoretical mechanisms that need further exploration.

5 Extended Model

As we take a multiple goals perspective, our starting point is the modified core model delineated earlier, which suggests that shifts of attention across multiple goals are more complex than Cyert and March (1963) originally contemplated. It retains sequential attention to goals as a mechanism that enables coping with bounded rationality but suggests that managers follow different sequences depending on whether their concern is to improve overall performance (problem-solving orientation) or to maintain a favorable self-image (self-enhancement orientation). Under a problem-solving orientation, they focus their attention on goals high in the goal hierarchy and move their attention down the hierarchy when goals that are the focus of attention are met. This implies that, when goals high in the goal hierarchy show a performance gap, search for new solutions is undertaken and change is implemented. Under a self-enhancement orientation, instead, managers give priority to goals on which performance is favorable. They neglect low performance on a goal high in the goal hierarchy when another goal of lesser importance is showing high performance, thus resulting in decreased responsiveness to low performance on goals that are high in the goal hierarchy. Similarly, attention shifts vertically toward goals in which performance is below aspirations when managers have a problem-solving orientation but shifts vertically toward goals with a favorable performance when they have a self-enhancement orientation. These horizontal and vertical shifts are predictable as long as we can model the managerial orientation. Taking this contrast between the problem-solving orientation and self-enhancement orientation as our starting point, we seek to identify conditions and mechanisms at the individual, organizational, and environmental levels that influence which orientation prevails in shaping responsiveness to multiple goals.

5.1 Individual Level

We begin by developing the individual-level component of such an extended model by identifying three key features that influence how decision-makers respond to multiple goals: personal involvement, ambiguity, and power. Our analysis suggests that self-enhancing responses to multiple goals are most likely when these three features have high values. Low values on any one of these three features put a brake on self-enhancing responses and make a problem-solving response more likely. After we specify this individual component of the model, we build on it to propose how the organizational hierarchy and features of the external environment impact the prevalence of a self-enhancement or problem-solving orientation among subunit managers and top managers.

5.1.1 Personal Involvement

Analyses of organizational responses to performance feedback generally assume that the individuals who participate in the decision-making process are those who initiated the activities that resulted in performance outcomes. In actual organizational decision-making, however, "participants come and go" (Cohen, March, and Olsen, 1972: 3). An implication of these movements is that the degree of personal involvement in the activities that result in performance outcomes among those who participate in the decision-making process may vary. Not only may people be new in their positions but responses to performance feedback may be impacted by participants in the decision-making process who have varying degrees of personal involvement due to differences in their roles. Personal involvement influences whether people respond to multiple goals by taking a problem-solving or a self-enhancement orientation because it carries implications of the performance outcomes for people's self-images. Self-enhancing response to performance feedback require personal involvement. When personal involvement is limited, decision-makers do not perceive unfavorable outcomes as a threat to their self-image. Lacking this threat, they are likely to adopt a problem-solving orientation that entails forming unbiased assessments of information that may be damaging.

For example, Kunda (1987) manipulated personal involvement in the lab by creating a connection between knowledge about a health threat and the personal situations of individuals. People who did not have a connection (low caffeine consumers) to the health threat (link between caffeine and a disease) did not show a tendency to self-enhance by questioning the truth of the health threat, whereas those who had a connection to the health threat (heavy caffeine consumers) were more likely to question the truth of the health threat. Additional support for the importance of personal involvement comes from a meta-analysis of experimental studies of self-threat (Campbell and Sedikides, 1999), which reports that self-threat is present among actors – participants who performed a task and received success or failure feedback – but not among observers – participants who observed another person receiving feedback.

A study of the assessment of creative work (Berg, 2016) points to the importance of roles that vary in the degree of personal involvement as a condition influencing self-enhancement. The study finds that creators overestimate the quality of their ideas, whereas managers form accurate assessment. Additional evidence supporting the importance of personal involvement comes from the literature on the escalation of commitment, which reveals that personal involvement in an investment decision triggers the tendency to stick to a course of action in the face of negative outcomes (Staw, 1976; Staw, Barsade, and

Koput, 1997). Those who take over the decision-making process from others who initiated it are less likely to "escalate," that is, they invest less in a course of action that receives negative feedback.

If people who are new in a position are less threatened by the poor outcomes of decisions that others made before them, the implication for responsiveness to multiple goals is that they are more likely to be guided by a problem-solving orientation whereby they respond to low performance on goals that are high in the goal hierarchy. Likewise, individuals who take an evaluative role in the decision-making process, like the managers in Berg's study, are less likely to shift attention across goals on the basis of the favorability of the outcomes and more likely to accurately assess negative feedback and favor actions that tackle performance gaps.

Although personal involvement generally activates self-enhancing responses to performance on multiple goals, we highlight two conditions that limit this effect and prompt a problem-solving orientation. Both conditions stem from the view that there are limits to people's discretion to form favorable assessments that help them maintain a positive self-image. According to the theory about self-enhancement, people self-enhance only if they think that their idiosyncratic interpretations of evaluative information are plausible in the eyes of a dispassionate observer (Kunda, 1990). In other words, the concern for maintaining or elevating their self-image is limited by the rival concern for being seen by others as credible. As we discuss later, the limit to self-enhancement posed by this concern for being seen by others as credible is altered by features of the environment of organizations that are currently high on the research agenda of organizational theorists. Aside from these environmental influences that we include in the extended model, there are instances in which decision-makers display delusional behaviors and cognitions (Chadwick, 1992). The theory of self-enhancement loses its predictive power in those extreme cases, but otherwise the credibility concern limits self-enhancement.

5.1.2 Ambiguity

At the individual level, the concern for being seen by others as credible is tightly linked to the ambiguity of the evaluative information, which is the first condition we propose limiting the influence of personal involvement on the activation of a self-enhancement orientation. Information that is clearly specified in its meaning and that is therefore low in ambiguity can't be easily dismissed. On the other hand, information that is open to a variety of interpretations enables people to use their own criteria to specify what is left unclear. Early evidence regarding the link between ambiguity and motivational orientation comes from studies that allow participants to self-evaluate on dimensions that vary in their degree of specificity (Felson, 1981; Dunning, Meyerowitz, and Holzberg, 1989). When the dimension is vaguely defined (e.g., being sensitive), participants are more likely to rate themselves favorably than when the dimension has an unequivocal meaning (e.g., being punctual). Individuals also take steps to introduce the ambiguity that enables them to self-enhance. When participants are given the opportunity to define dimensions on which to self-evaluate are initially vague, self-enhancing evaluations are more likely when they are allowed to pick more criteria to define dimensions, which suggests that they define vague dimensions in ways that enable them to highlight their strengths (Dunning et al., 1989). Ambiguity alone is not sufficient to prompt favorable assessments of performance. It requires the personal involvement of decision-makers that establishes a link between negative assessments and threats to the self-image. When this link is absent, ambiguity can be used by evaluators for the opposite motivational end such as when it strengthens negative biases regarding the ability of others (Heilman, Block, Stathatos, 1997).

In the context of performance assessment, ambiguity that elevates self-enhancing response to feedback may arise from a variety of sources including inconsistent aspiration levels (Joseph and Gaba, 2015), idiosyncratic comparison groups (Audia, Brion, and Greve, 2015), and atypical organizational identities (Smith and Chae, 2017). A key source of ambiguity particularly relevant to our model stems from the multiplicity of goals. As we discussed earlier, the organization as a whole and its subunits pursue myriad of goals. When performance is low on more than one goal, ambiguity is reduced and consequently, the theory holds, it is difficult to form favorable interpretations that are credible. A problem-solving orientation prevails in those situations unless the situation is so dire that survival becomes a dominant concern. But when performance is high on some goals and low on others, opportunities arise for forming defensible favorable interpretations that generally hinge on giving more weight to the goals denoting positive outcomes and downplaying goals evidencing poor outcomes (Audia and Brion, 2007). So thus far the individual component of the model suggests that personal involvement coupled with ambiguity prompts self-enhancement responses to performance on multiple goals. Conversely, low personal involvement as well as high personal involvement coupled with low ambiguity prompts problem-solving responses to performance on multiple goals.

5.1.3 Power

The amount of power decision-makers possess is another important influence on the extent to which decision-makers adopt a self-enhancement orientation or a problem-solving orientation when responding to performance on multiple goals. An extensive body of work suggests and shows that power impacts the extent to which individuals focus on their internal states and on social norms

(Keltner et al. 2003; Guinote, 2017). Because high-power individuals are accustomed to get what they want with little interference, they are generally more focused on the pursuit of valued rewards than on determining and meeting others' expectations. In other words, their pursuit of valued rewards reduces their inhibition. When considering whether self-enhancing interpretations of low performance are plausible in the eyes of dispassionate observers, high-power decision-makers may overlook the views of these observers and thus downplay their potential disapproval. Conversely, low-power individuals spend significantly more time assessing social norms as they strive to conform to them to gain social approval. Their vigilance of social norms strengthens the perceived constraints posed by the views of others. So, when personal involvement is high and ambiguity of evaluative information is high, this difference between high- and low-power individuals alters their response to multiple goals. Because their main focus is on internal states, high-power individuals will feel unconstrained by the views of others as they revise the goal hierarchy to form self-enhancing interpretations of performance on multiple goals. On the other hand, low power attenuates self-enhancement because it prompts decision-makers to refrain from favorable interpretations of performance that they perceive will cause others' disapproval. Our model thus suggests that, under conditions of high personal involvement and low ambiguity, low-power individuals are more inclined than high-power individuals to adopt a problem-solving orientation than a self-enhancement orientation when responding to performance on multiple goals.

While research looking at responsiveness to multiple goals is still limited, some evidence supportive of the view that high power makes a self-enhancing orientation more likely comes from Blagoeva et al. (2020), who find that firms led by CEOs who possess more power make R&D decisions that are less sensitive to performance declines on a primary goal. Focusing on how performance is assessed, Audia, Brion, and Rousseau (2021) report that firms led by more powerful CEOs are more likely to create comparison groups that diverge from what external actors consider appropriate and more likely to do so when performance on a primary goal deteriorates.

5.1.4 Conclusion

The individual level is where the contrast between problem-solving and self-enhancing orientations to performance feedback gets personal. Consider the decision-maker facing performance below the aspiration level, meaning performance below either that of peers or below earlier performance, or both. Becoming an organizational decision-maker with a goal and performance feedback (possibly multiple goals) is a significant career stage, regardless of the organizational level, because organizational positions involving decisions important enough to trace and report performance outcomes are gained through promotion or certification. When performance below the aspiration level is perceived as a personal threat, decision-makers may switch from a problem-solving to a self-enhancement orientation. Our extended model specifies personal involvement, ambiguity, and power as key situational characteristics that channel the individual response into either problem-solving or self-enhancement. This means that the individual response is not determined by the person or consistent over time; it is guided by situational factors.

The individual orientation is consequential for the organization. Organizations have goals and report performance because they seek to identify problems and control the rate of organizational change. Change is costly and risky. So, if decision-makers can be regulated to make changes only when the status quo leads to worse outcomes, the organization may be better off. In a world of bounded rationality and limited foresight, it is not reasonable to expect that performance feedback will reliably produce this outcome. For example, the decreased responsiveness to low performance that results from a self-enhancement orientation may allow an individual to persist on a course of action that ultimately produces value for the organization. Accordingly, we cannot say whether the self-enhancing decision-maker is worse for the organization than the problem-solving one at any given time. We can predict that the self-enhancing decision-maker is less likely to initiate change as a result of undertaking less search for solutions. According to the extended model we develop here, the personal involvement, the degree of ambiguity, and the power structure let us predict organizational change with significant precision. What remains is to test whether this model holds true empirically.

The individual-level component of the model lays out basic mechanisms that specify likely behavioral responses by decision-makers charged with the task of responding to performance on goals. But decision-making in organizations is not a solitary activity undertaken by isolated individuals (Cyert and March, 1963). The organizational context that most directly impinges on the day-to-day activities of decision-makers alters the way these mechanisms influence their behavior. Analyses of responsiveness of performance on multiple goals must therefore take into account additional influences stemming from the context. We highlight the varying influences of the context by focusing on two key groups of actors: subunit managers and top managers.

5.2 Organizational Level

Starting with Cyert and March (1963), much of the organizational literature on performance feedback views the organizational hierarchy as consisting of two hierarchical levels: the organizational level and the subunit level. At the organizational level, top managers[2] are responsible for achieving organizational goals and responding to performance on those goals by making changes to the strategy and administrative structure of the entire organization. Top managers also decompose organizational goals into goals assigned to subunits and develop control systems aimed at achieving coordination among subunits. Subunit managers have narrower job domains as they are expected to coordinate activities within subunits, pursue subunit goals, and adjust their behavior in response to performance on such goals. The administrative mechanisms used by top managers to coordinate and control organizational activities are an important influence on how subunit managers assess and respond to performance on multiple subunit goals.

Building on the individual component of the extended model we outlined earlier, we identify two features of the formal organization that alter subunit managers' propensity to adopt a self-enhancement or problem-solving orientation: the centralization of subunit decisions and the formalization of subunit performance evaluation. Both limit self-enhancement and make a problem-solving response to performance on multiple goals more likely. Centralization of subunit decisions weakens the link between subunit low performance and self-threat to the people participating in decision-making, whereas formalization of subunit performance evaluation reduces ambiguity, thereby limiting decision-makers' latitude to form interpretations of performance that are credible in the eyes of others. We also identify one feature of the informal organization that alters subunit managers' choice of orientation: the power of their subunit. Regardless of the formal authority relations and processes for managing these, power is distributed unequally in organizations and affects subunit managers' compliance with the formal authority (Salancik and Pfeffer, 1974; Pfeffer, 1981).

5.2.1 Centralization

The degree of centralization of subunit decisions captures the extent to which top managers participate in decisions regarding subunit activities (Pugh et al., 1968). In decentralized structures, the locus of authority for decisions concerning subunit activities resides within the subunit. Subunit managers are accountable to top managers for the subunit outcomes but act independently, making most decisions with little or no involvement of the upper echelon. Because of their high personal involvement in the activities of the subunit, the link between

---

[2] We are aware that it is currently fashionable to refer to top managers as executives (Mautner and Learmonth, 2020). For clarity in exposition, we use the simpler distinction between top managers and subunit managers.

low performance on a goal high in the hierarchy of goals of the subunit and threat to the self-image is strong. As proposed in the individual-level component of the model, to maintain a positive self-image, subunit managers are likely to form favorable assessments of performance by switching attention to goals that are lower in the goal hierarchy of the subunit but that evidence positive outcomes.

In centralized structures, in contrast, top managers routinely participate in decisions that impact subunit activities. Their participation may range from selective involvement in decision made together with subunit managers, as described by Joseph, Klingebiel, and Wilson's (2016) study of product phase-out or Sengul and Gimeno's (2013) analysis of subsidiaries' constrained discretion in multi-market firms, to total control of subunit decisions, as in Siggelkow and Levinthal's (2003) simulation model and Mintzberg's (1979) simple structures. Compared to subunit managers, top managers generally do not view low performance on an important subunit goal as a threat to their self-image because they are less likely than subunit managers to be among those who initiate activities in the subunits. Indeed, much of their efforts are oriented toward coordinating and integrating activities across subunits. Consequently, problems evidenced by low performance at the subunit level are less directly tied to assessments of their own performance, which instead depends on the combined results of multiple subunits and encompasses the entire organization. If the link between low performance and self-threat activates self-enhancement and low subunit performance is not a threat to the self-image of top managers, then, according to this model, top managers participating in subunit decisions are more likely to adopt a problem-solving orientation. Accordingly, they are more inclined to respond to low performance on goals that are high in the goal hierarchy of the subunit and less predisposed to shift attention to subunit goals that evidence positive outcomes but are lower in the goal hierarchy.

Top managers do not have to voice their views when subunit decisions are being made for a problem-solving orientation to prevail. Their participation, in fact, may serve as a mental watchdog for subunit managers. Awareness of top managers' likely positions on a performance issue may prompt subunit managers to conform to those views, thereby curtailing self-enhancement and elevating their propensity to adopt a problem-solving orientation in response to multiple subunit goals (Tetlock, Skitka, and Boettger, 1989; Park, Westphal, and Stern, 2011). Following this reasoning, a problem-solving orientation in the responsiveness to multiple goals by subunit managers is likely to be more pronounced when the organization adopts a centralized approach to subunit decisions. Evidence supporting the influence of centralization on responsiveness to performance comes from Joseph, Klingebiel, and Wilson (2016) who report that centralized firms drop products in response to low performance on a single goal significantly more than decentralized firms.

5.2.2 Formalization

Subunit managers are also constrained in their responses to performance on multiple goals by the degree of formalization of the evaluation of subunit performance. Formalization is the extent to which an organization uses formal procedures to prescribe and assess behavior (Pugh et al., 1968). These procedures concern what needs to be done, how to evaluate outcomes, and how to respond to poor and negative outcomes through discipline and rewards (Edwards, 1979). Importantly, it is not just the existence of formal procedures that impacts managerial discretion but the extent to which they are clearly articulated. Indeed, Edelman (1992) reports that procedures that leave ample room for interpretation allow managers to exercise considerable discretion in the way they are implemented. Research on pay inequity reports a similar pattern, indicating that procedures that specify with precision how rewards should be assigned are more effective in eradicating managerial bias (Elvira and Graham, 2002).

Discretion is critical in the way a self-enhancing response to performance feedback manifests itself. It may entail revising the priority of goals, which is central in our analysis of multiple goals, but also increasing the level of abstraction of goals, and invoking counterfactual outcomes as comparison standards (Jordan and Audia, 2012). It is easier to make these after-the-fact adjustments that allow decision-makers to form favorable assessments of low performance when procedures for the assessment of performance are poorly defined or completely lacking. As we outlined earlier, decision-makers who put forward idiosyncratic assessments of performance to maintain a positive self-image do so only to the extent that they perceive these interpretations to be plausible and credible in the eyes of others. The degree of formalization of the evaluation of subunit performance greatly reduces the discretion that enables self-enhancement by making it easier for dispassionate observers – in this case, top managers – to identify interpretations that cross a red line. Govindarajan (1988), for example, examines multiunit firms that evaluate the performance of subunits on the basis of profits even when other metrics such as the quality of products may be equally valuable indicators of performance. Similarly, Mazmanian and Beckman (2018) give a detailed account of a highly formalized process by which a hotel management company sets a net revenue goal for its units. In such a formalized process, once the goal is set, a manager says, "it becomes gospel" (Mazmanian and Beckman (2018: 364). Other goals such as profitability, growth, or customer satisfaction are out of the picture. In this way, the unequivocal specification of a metric in a performance evaluation procedure becomes a deterrent to revisions of the goal hierarchy that subunit managers may contemplate in response to low performance on the net revenue goal. Therefore, at the level of the subunit, we anticipate variations in how subunit managers respond to multiple goals as a function of the degree of formalization of performance evaluation of the subunit. In organizations that formalize the performance evaluation procedure, subunit unit managers will be more likely to respond to performance on multiple goals by adopting a problem-solving orientation.

5.2.3 Power

While centralization and formalization constrain subunit managers' propensity to self-enhance when they respond to performance on multiple goals, the power of subunit managers may serve as a countervailing force. The individual component of the model suggests that power makes individuals more focused on the pursuit of rewards and less concerned about the dissenting views of others. Together, these consequences of power prompt powerful subunit managers to feel less encumbered by the participation in decision-making of top managers and by the formalization of evaluation of subunit performance. Research on subunit power found early on that more powerful subunits were able to accumulate valued resources and were less likely to change when facing low performance (Salancik and Pfeffer, 1974; Manns and March, 1978). Later work has supported these findings and also suggested that the subunit power is remarkably rigid. Boeker (1989) reported that subunit power originating in its importance for a given environment was maintained over time even if the environment changed. A leading cause of loss in subunit power was low organizational performance, perhaps implying that a powerful subunit manager engaging in self-enhancement rather than problem-solving gradually undermines the subunit power.

The power of subunit managers may also influence top managers. Powerful subunits' influence on corporate decisions and the corporate agenda may deter top managers from strict enforcement of internal control processes (Gaba and Joseph, 2013). This implies that, in organizations with centralized decision-making, top managers participating in subunit decision-making may tone down their voices when they interact with managers of powerful subunits. Similarly, in organizations with a greater degree of formalization, top managers may make exceptions to the application of procedures for the evaluation of performance when evaluating powerful subunit managers. Indeed, some of the earliest findings on organizational responses to low performance suggest a role of subunit power. Manns and March (1978) found that university departments with high power made less curriculum change in response to financial adversity, a finding echoed by Gaba and Joseph (2013), who found that large divisions of a corporation had more freedom to choose their responses to performance below the aspiration level.

5.2.4 Conclusion

At the organization level, the individual effects on problem-solving versus self-enhancing orientations operate at a larger scale. The consequences are more significant because the theory at this level addresses the behavior of subunit managers, whereas the individual-level theory applies to any individual making decisions in response to performance on multiple goals. Organizational changes at the subunit level are costly and risky, and they are more likely to be interdependent with other organizational subunits, increasing the uncertainty of the consequences. Whether performance feedback regulates the rate and type of change correctly is an even more significant question at this level of analysis, and again, we are better able to predict what orientation makes more changes than whether the higher rate of change resulting from a problem-solving orientation actually solves the organizational problems well.

The causes at this level are organizational structures and power relations, with centralization, formalization, and subunit power channeling the decision-maker into either a problem-solving or a self-enhancing orientation. The reason for selecting these three is that the extended model we specify connects the individual and organizational levels of analysis. Centralization and formalization operate through their effect on personal involvement and ambiguity. Subunit power operates because it is a source of personal power. The decision-maker at the individual level is personally threatened by performance below aspiration levels, and for the subunit manager we analyze here the threat and the credibility of favorable assessments is altered by organizational factors. Because other factors that connect the two levels could have the same effects, the extended model we specify is likely incomplete. Nonetheless, we believe that these three factors are the ones that connect the organizational level to the individual level in the most straightforward way, and hence should be the first targets for empirical investigation.

5.3 Environment Level

Continuing to build on the individual component of the model, we now turn to an analysis of how the environment influences an organization's responsiveness to multiple goals. Our focus is on variations in environmental influences that alter the degree of ambiguity of environmental demands and in so doing enable or constrain top managers' self-enhancing responses to multiple goals thereby making a problem-solving orientation more likely. We start by drawing on institutional research that views environments as potentially consisting of multiple logics. The concept of logics is important as we seek to develop a theoretical perspective on multiple goals because it ties cultural constructions that infuse organizational behaviors with meaning to the process by which organizations define and pursue goals. We continue by noting that the environment also differs in the formalization of performance assessment, which influences the managerial ability to engage in self-enhancement. Finally, organizational power relative to the environment has similar effects as subunit power relative to the top management, as it allows the organizational top management to disregard some of the influence that the environment gains from having clearly defined and formalized goals and external assessment.

5.3.1 Logics

A logic prescribes what constitutes appropriate behavior including what goals are appropriate and necessary (Thornton and Ocasio, 1999; Thornton, 2001, 2002). Conforming to a logic is a means by which organizations understand the social world and secure support from important referent audiences that adhere to that logic (Suddaby and Greenwood, 2005). For example, microfinance organizations that confront a development logic infer from it the importance of pursuing the goal of helping the poor (Battilana and Dorado, 2010). Similarly, large for-profit corporations that face a sustainability logic consider the goal of protecting the environment as an important component of their mission (Hoffman, 1999), and university departments that embrace the logic of academic science view the goal of producing publications as the predominant means of pursuing knowledge for knowledge's sake (Owen-Smith and Powell, 2001). Importantly, the logics are not always stable and simple. Organizations face environments in which logics change over time, as when the publishing industry moved from an editorial logic to a commercial logic (Thornton and Ocasio, 1999), but they also face institutionally complex environments characterized by the coexistence of multiple logics (Friedland and Alford, 1991). The fragmentation of the environment organizations face is an important source of institutional complexity (Greenwood et al., 2011). Fragmentation refers to the number of social actors on which organizations depend. Whereas in unified fields organization face a few external actors, in fragmented fields the coexistence of multiple actors and their respective logics increases the variety of institutional expectations organizations face. This creates ambiguity that, according to our model, enables decision-makers to form self-enhancing assessments of performance on multiple goals.

Top managers concerned with satisfying goals that reflect multiple logics have opportunities to form favorable interpretations of the overall performance when performance on an important goal embedded in an influential logic is poor. They can give greater attention to goals that reflect a different logic. The fact that the goal on which performance is positive is embedded in a distinct logic confers credibility to the self-enhancing assessment and helps to garner support from the institutional referents endorsing that logic. For example, in environments in which firms confront both a market logic and a sustainability logic, they have greater latitude to form favorable assessments of performance when market goals are not met by shifting attention to their conformity with the sustainability logic. In essence, institutional complexity, which is often seen as a source of strain for organizations (e.g., Pache and Santos, 2010), may turn into a potential advantage for their top managers. Seeking to conform to rules of what is appropriate emanating from different logics requires effort and resources, but these efforts afford top managers with greater opportunities to maintain an image of competence when performance on some of the goals reflecting other logics deteriorate. Our view that institutional complexity enables self-enhancing response to performance on multiple goals is consistent with the work of institutional theorists who depict individuals as retaining some autonomy as they respond to institutional constraints. Exemplifying this position, Thornton, Ocasio, and Lounsbury (2012: 83) note that "given the availability of multiple logics, individuals have the potential for agency in choosing which of the multiple logics they rely on for social action and interaction (Friedland and Alford, 1991)".

The potential for self-enhancement inherent in multiple logics is only part of the story, however, because organizations' adherence to values and beliefs underlying a specific logic may be constrained by internal and external factors. Internally, logics may gain support because they reflect political or cultural views of organizational members (Lounsbury, 2001; Briscoe, Chin, and Hambrick, 2014). Externally, logics are imposed with greater force when their proponents can influence key actors such as customers or legal authorities (Purdy and Gray, 2009; Sauder and Espeland, 2009). Complex institutional environments with multiple logics imply organizational choices because the logics impose contradictory claims on organizational actions or resources, and organizations may not have the capacity necessary to decouple these (Meyer and Rowan, 1977). As a result, organizations are drawn into specific logics depending on their social position. Organizational decision-makers, in turn, will seek to maneuver the goals and performance feedback from each logic as best they can, and ironically the organizational constraints that stem from multiple logics may result into managerial freedom to self-enhance.

5.3.2 Formalization

Besides their fragmentation, environments also vary in the extent to which they prescribe formalized procedures to determine what constitutes organizational success or failure. Meyer, Scott, and Strang (1987: 190), for example, chronicle changes in externally generated procedures for determining the effectiveness of schools. They report that schools dependent on local community funding were subject to vaguely defined conceptions of effectiveness but, as funding from the state expanded, these conceptions of effectiveness became "more clear, better specified, more uniform," ultimately leading to the use of standardized tests for the evaluation of schools and school systems. Externally generated measures of environmental performance offer another example. Whereas measures such as ISO 14001 Environment Management System Standard consist of a plan to work on protecting the environment that lacks specific measurement of outcomes (Delmas and Toffel, 2008), external ratings of corporate social performance such as those created by KLD Research Analytics specify distinct performance dimensions, data gathering procedures, and evaluation methods (Chatterji and Toffel, 2010). The level of formalization of these externally imposed goals is clearly different, and it will affect organizational responses.

In our extended model this formalization of externally prescribed goals impacts top managers in the same way that the formalization of the procedures for determining subunit performance impacts subunit managers. It forces top managers to acknowledge and respond to low performance on goals thereby making a problem-solving response to performance on multiple goals more likely. Just like top managers who control subunits, referent audiences monitor organizational progress toward goals and discipline organizations that fail to meet those goals (Sauder and Espeland 2009). Aware of these external formalized procedures of evaluation, top managers refrain from redefining unfavorable performance in positive ways because they view such self-enhancing behavior as not credible in the eyes of external actors. The following quote of a law school's dean experience of external ratings illustrates how formally defined external measures of performance force organizations to acknowledge external assessments while clamping down on instinctive tendencies to put forward favorable assessments: "I live in dread fear that we will fall to the fourth tier on my watch. That's ridiculous! We're a wonderful law school" (Sauder and Espeland, 2009: 69).

The vague specification of what constitutes achieving an externally pre-scribed goal that characterize environments with low formalization of evalu-ation procedures attenuates this constraint as it gives top managers room for forming plausible interpretations they can defend. So, whereas firms show significant discretion in whether to respond to externally generated evaluations of performance that are vaguely defined (Rowley et al., 2017), they are likely to take actions to fix low performance evidenced by external evaluations that are clearly specified (Chatterji and Toffel, 2010).

5.3.3 Power

Just as the power of subunit managers may modify the impact of centralization and formalization on how they respond to multiple subunit goals, we expect that the power possessed by top managers will alter the influence of institu-tional complexity and formalization of externally generated performance assessments on how they respond to performance on multiple organizational goals. As we outlined in the individual component of the model, individuals who possess power are used to pursuing things they value without letting others' views act as deterrent to action. In our extended model, this orientation coupled with low inhibition exacerbates high power top managers' propensity to engage in self-enhancing responses to performance on goals tied to differ-ent logics. At the same time, these psychological consequences of power make top managers less sensitive to the constraining effect of formalized external assessments and thus more inclined to let self-enhancement be the motive guiding responsiveness to multiple goals.

Work in resource dependence theory points to ways in which top managers acquire power in relation to other firms. It views organizations as seeking to avoid dependence on others and as engaging in a broad range of activities to avoid responding to environmental demands (Pfeffer and Salancik, 1978). This is done through defense mechanisms such as coopting external actors by giving board memberships to top managers of influential organizations (Burt, Christman, and Kilburn, 1980; Hillman, Withers, and Collins, 2009) including sources of finance (Davis and Mizruchi, 1999), politicians (Hillman, 2005), and state representatives (Zhang and Greve, 2018). Alliances have a similar role, as they impose interorganizational constraints (Gulati and Gargiulo, 1999). The behavioral perspective advanced in our model suggests that these interorganizational relationships are not simply structural constraints that limit organizational ability to adapt to changes in the environment but also sources of power that alter the way top managers assess performance on multiple goals making them more inclined to adopt a self-enhancement orientation and thus disregard evidence of poor performance.

The influence of power in giving top managers the choice of engaging in self-enhancement rather than problem-solving in response to performance below aspiration levels may be part of the explanation for the many cases of firms with leading technologies and market power experiencing sudden downfalls in the face of disruptive technological change. Much attention has been given to top management inability to understand technological change and formulate responses to it (e.g., Tushman and Anderson, 1986; Tripsas, 2009; Benner and Tripsas, 2012), and this mechanism is no doubt influential. What this argument misses, however, is the distinction between being unable to anticipate the effects of technological change and being unable to respond to technological change. Firms that see their technological and market advantages undermined by a new technology will go through a period of low performance that could give rise to problem-solving and recovery, as has occurred for some firms in some markets (Sosa, 2011). Many of the markets with the most dramatic downfalls have in common that the incumbent firms were very powerful, and accordingly had managers who may have engaged in self enhancement rather than problem-solving. To take some prominent firms from the literature, cement firms have regional monopolies, aircraft makers and minicomputer makers were oligopolies (Tushman and Anderson, 1986), the few camera makers before digital cameras had expensive and distinct competencies (Tripsas, 2009), and hard disk makers with standardized formats had significant scale economies (Christensen and Bower, 1996). In each case, the power of incumbent firms seemed sufficiently great to allow its top managers to indulge in self-enhancing assessments of performance on multiple goals.

5.3.4 Conclusion

At the environmental level, the effects operate at a yet larger scale, as we are now specifying an extended model of organizational performance feedback – organization-level goals and performance – and how organizational responses are affected by environmental characteristics. This is a familiar level of analysis because most evidence of performance feedback involves organization-level goals such as profitability, market share, growth, product safety, and the like. Yet, the extended model is still novel because it predicts how logics, formalization, and power modify responses to performance on multiple goals by channeling the decision-maker into a problem-solving or self-enhancing orientation. In its basic form, the decision-maker has a problem-solving orientation when environmental prescriptions of what goals are regarded as appropriate stem from a single logic, external evaluations of performance are formalized, and the organization has insufficient power to disregard the views of external actors. Under those restrictive conditions, the extended model applied to top managers collapses into the modified model because the additional considerations discussed in this Element are absent. Inside the organization, the extended model would still apply unless any interpretive space to form favorable assessments at the subunit level is eliminated by high degrees of formalization of the evaluation of subunit performance.

By connecting individual-level mechanisms to features of the organizational and environmental context, the extended model implies cross-level predictions as well. Compared to subunit managers, top managers of an organization have a more ambiguous set of goals that are not ranked and assessed as easily as intraorganizational goals. Many logics and low environmental formalization do not directly increase personal involvement, but they give top management room to question the relevance of a goal for which the organization is currently performing poorly. The power effect may also differ across levels as top managers, taking on the mantle of organizational power, can introduce new criteria by which their performance is assessed and resist environmental pressures with greater ease than a manager of a powerful subunit can resist the direct superiors.

In an organization, the conditions that regulate a decision-maker's orientation are to some extent designed, and so are those that regulate a subunit manager's orientation. Although it would be surprising if personal involvement, decentralization, and formalization were designed to reliably generate organizational change exactly when the benefits exceed the cost and risk, it is at least conceivable that an organization can gradually adjust its systems to improve its goal structure and other decision-making characteristics. For the environmental effects, this is simply not the case. Logics are imposed, formalization is imposed, and the power (or lack of dependence) that the organization seeks is exactly what can prevent it from engaging in a problem-solving orientation. One reason organization theory is so focused on environmental conditions holds true for our extended model too: they are nearly uncontrollable and very consequential. The environmental component of the extended model describes how organizations may end up in a problem-solving orientation when they are better off unchanged, or in a self-enhancement orientation when they need to change, or perhaps will have the orientation that is appropriate for their situation. The actions taken by the organization are consequential, making research to understand the orientation and the resulting change, or lack of change, important for our theoretical and empirical progress.

5.4 Full Extended Model

Figure 2 illustrates the extended model in simplified form. As the figure shows, performance on multiple goals can result in a problem-solving response or a self-enhancing response, and individual, organizational, and environmental factors influence which type of response is more likely. Seeing these two types of responses as mutually exclusive at all times is a simplification since decision-makers in organizations are capable of engaging in problem-solving and self-enhancing actions at once. Indeed, even a manager who fully intends to engage in a self-enhancing reaction to performance feedback may undertake a problemistic search as a form of cover. After all, examining alternatives is the best way to argue that the current set of actions is the best choice, and that all other choices would have given even worse performance than the current. A subunit manager making such a presentation in a formalized and centralized organization may succeed and sometimes be able to engage in self-enhancement (contrary to our prediction), but may also fail and be forced to make changes, or may even be replaced by someone else.

As the figure shows, other elements of the modified model are still in place, with the survival point weakening the relation between problem-solving response and organizational change. The kinked-curve relation is produced by the survival point and self-enhancement, and does not need to be shown separately. A self-enhancing response means less change than one would observe if a problem-solving response prevailed but it is not the same as rigidity. A manager who seeks to self-enhance might be making changes that are symbolic and also changes that are seen as supplementary to past actions rather than as rejections. How to identify the subtle ways in which self-enhancement might become manifest will require additional efforts to those we have deployed here. Longitudinal analyses of firms are often best suited for capturing the binary relation of change versus no change, missing the element of interpretation that skillful managers exploit when showing

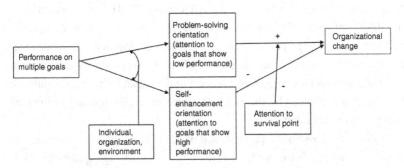

Figure 2 Extended model of performance feedback

that they are changing, but in ways that demonstrate that the past actions were correct even though performance was below the aspiration level. We will discuss the research opportunities that the extended model opens up in Section 7, but first we use Section 6 to give a practical example of organizational behavior that is best understood using its concepts and relations.

6 An Example

To illustrate what responsiveness to multiple goals looks like in an organizational context and also to offer examples of some of the components of the extended model we look at Random House Trade Publishing Group (RHTPG), a unit of Bertelsmann's Random House Inc. (RHI), between 1998 and 2002 (Anand, Rukstad, and Kostring, 2005; Anand, Barnett, and Carpenter, 2007). During this period Ann Godoff was the president, publisher, and editor in chief of RHTPG. Her boss was Peter Olson, the chief executive officer of RHI. They were appointed to these positions around the same time, late 1997 and early 1998. Godoff had a background in publishing, whereas Olson had a background in banking and finance (Kolker, 2001).

Two distinct institutional logics influenced how publishing was approached by industry insiders (Thornton and Ocasio, 1999). The editorial logic viewed the industry as primarily a cultural enterprise focused on promoting the circulation of ideas in a democratic society through the publication of high-quality books. This logic prescribed goals related to the quality of the work published such as the number of books on bestseller lists, the development of new big-name authors, and a strong reputation in publisher-academic circles. The market logic emphasized the importance of achieving a financial return on the resources invested. It viewed publishing as a business enterprise and quantified success through profits.

Scholars who trace the relative influence of these two logics over time identify the late 1980s as the period in which the market logic supplanted the editorial logic as the dominant cultural lens through which the industry was understood (Thornton and Ocasio, 1999; Thornton, 2004). But despite this shift in relative influence, the editorial logic did not vanish overnight. In an organizational analysis of responsiveness to multiple goals, logics persist to the extent that the goals they prescribe continue to influence how performance is assessed and the decisions they trigger. At the level of the subunit, the relative influence of a logic is evidenced by the extent to which managers respond to the goals prescribed by that logic.

Godoff could assess the performance of RHTPG on goals that captured the quality of the published work such as the number of high-quality books on bestsellers' lists and also on goals that were more financial in nature such as operating profit or profitability expressed as a percentage of sales (Anand et al., 2007). Between 1998 and 2002, her unit performed very poorly on financial goals but achieved considerable success on publishing quality goals. Regarding the financial results, one source reports that RHTPG accumulated losses for a total of $10 million (Kelly, 2003), whereas another refers to RHTPG being the only unit within RHI "consistently falling short of profitability targets" (Kirkpatrick, 2003). On the editorial quality side, notable achievements included several books by unknown authors that became major bestsellers, more bestsellers than any other division inside RHI, growing reputation in the close-knit community of literary agents, and an expanding roster of big-name literary authors (Kolker, 2001; Anand et al., 2007).

If she had adopted a problem-solving orientation to these performance outcomes, Godoff would have taken actions oriented to addressing the gap on the profitability goal. This would have meant making the unit more efficient by taking actions such as reducing costs and investing in marketing to expand sales. A self-enhancement orientation, on the other hand, would have implied a reluctance to take actions oriented to tackling the profitability gap and a continued emphasis on actions that strengthened the success on the publishing quality goals.

Godoff appeared to have responded to performance on multiple goals by adopting a self-enhancement orientation. First, low levels of profitability persisted during this period of time. If she had taken actions aimed at tackling the profitability gap, performance on the profit goal would have improved. Second, press coverage of her reputation within literary circles was glowing, but also reported that she made slow progress in expanding investments in marketing and the launch of a paperback product line (Kolker, 2001). Third, her lack of concern for profits was also evident in her increasing use of aggressive bidding against other divisions within RHI to sign big-name authors such as Salman Rushdie. According to one source "she was a big spender" (Kelly, 2003). Greater up-front payments negatively impacted the profitability of the unit. While profitability appeared to be an afterthought, Godoff continued to make her relationship with literary agents and big-name authors a primary focus. In a New York Magazine article (Kolker, 2001) evocatively titled "Waiting for Godoff," a not so subtle act of deference from the author of the piece, an impressive cast of luminaries praised Godoff for her influence on their work. This article also illustrates how the existence of multiple logics enabled a self-enhancing response. It is not simply that multiple logics prescribe different goals that may vary in terms of performance outcomes. They also reflect the way distinct referent audiences view publishing. Giving greater importance to the goal prescribed by the editorial logic enabled Godoff to benefit from the support of the academic-literary community adhering to that logic. The existence of a distinct logic aligned with the goals evidencing positive results lent credibility to Godoff's self-enhancing response.

Godoff's response to the multiple goals of editorial quality and profitability is consistent with the prediction of our model that subunit managers facing diverging performance on multiple goals are oriented to respond to the goal showing positive performance. Our model suggests three conditions that may have made this scenario more likely. The first is the low degree of centralization in the decisions made by RHTPG. Centralization reduces self-enhancement because top managers are less threatened by low performance on profitability than subunit manager due to their lower involvement in subunit activities and consequently are more inclined to focus on addressing performance gaps. But in this instance centralization was low. Peter Olson adopted a hands-off approach in dealing with division heads. He admitted "I do not get involved in the day-to-day activities. Publishing should not be managed from the top. I will not second guess a title, a cover, layout, or ad campaign" (Anand et al., 2007:10). He also encouraged internal competition as units were allowed to bid against each other for the rights for a particular book in an auction.

Our model also views a low degree of formalization of the assessment of the subunit performance as a condition that favors a self-enhancement response to performance on multiple goals. Between 1998 and 2002 the criteria to assess the performance of RHTPG were not clearly spelled out. Olson referred to the importance of meeting goals but he was vague in their specification. He used language commonly used by adherents of the market logic when he said "I set clear goals and I expect them (unit managers) to outperform the market" (Anand et al., 2007:10). But he also gave importance to less tangible aspects of publishing success when he said that he wanted "publishing to be life and death for the publishers ... I want it consuming their lives... I want them to feel the intoxication of success and the rush of getting on the New York Times best sellers list" (Anand et al., 2007: 10). Commenting specifically on Godoff, he also added ambiguity regarding the temporal dimension of performance when he observed that "Ann is really taking a long-term view of growing the division" (Kolker, 2001).

Our model also identifies the power of the subunit manager as a condition that strengthens a self-enhancement orientation, and Godoff appeared to possess considerable power within the organization. She had important allies within the organization that propelled her to her current position in a swift succession of promotions, the last of which involved replacing her former boss in November 1997 (Kolker, 2001). While internal promotions consolidated her position of authority, another key source of power stemmed from her glowing reputation among important writers and literary agents who took great pride in working with her (Kirkpatrick, 2003). It is not a surprise then that Godoff was perceived by many as "a sort of favorite child among the German ownership," which named all book operations around the globe Random House (Kolker, 2001).

Our extended model suggests that a change in any of these conditions could have altered the way in which the subunit responded to multiple goals. Although Godoff had her contract renewed during the summer of 2002, Olson abruptly fired her in January 2003, bringing to a halt the self-enhancing response to multiple goals shown over the previous four years and starting a period in which RHTPG adopted a problem-solving response in which addressing the profitability gap became a key priority. A key trigger for this decision appeared to have been the introduction of a more formalized process of subunit performance evaluation. In June 2002, Bertelsmann' top managers formulated criteria that would be used to reevaluate which business units to retain and which to divest. One of these criteria required that each division met clear performance targets using three measures: (1) return on sales targets; (2) return on invested capital greater than 10 percent after taxes; and (3) free cash flows that exceeded 100 percent of earnings before interest, taxes, and amortization (Anand et al., 2005).

For Godoff, this was clarity with consequences. These clearly delineated metrics eliminated the ambiguity that had allowed Godoff and her boss to downplay the profitability goal and to focus instead on the more vaguely defined editorial quality goal of RHPTG. A memo announcing Godoff's departure suggests that the greater precision with which subunit performance had to be assessed forced the change: "Despite the many publishing strengths of the Random House Trade Group and their numerous bestsellers, they have been the only Random House Inc. publishing division to consistently fall short of their annual profitability targets" (Kirkpatrick, 2003). Olson remarked in other public statements that "it was the toughest decision of my career" (Kelly, 2003), which suggests that the new rules to assess performance might have tilted the balance in favor a problem-solving orientation, no longer allowing Olson to ignore the subunit's self-enhancing response to performance now unambiguously diverging from the corporate's goal hierarchy.

7 Future Research

The extended model of performance feedback is meant as a guide toward research opportunities and a platform for building theory through the mechanisms we have posited. Although the details of this research will differ among papers because each will have its own configuration of theory, phenomenon, and data, we make some suggestions here for future research opportunities. These suggestions are incomplete because they are colored by our own experience and preferences and will omit anything outside our field of vision. We offer them as starting points.

Our first set of suggestions for future research is based on the extended model mechanisms in the three levels of analysis and is fundamental for testing whether these mechanisms modify the responses to performance feedback as the theory developed here specifies. If the findings are in line with our predictions, we will have a much better understanding of the origins of heterogeneity in organizational change (and non-change) to performance below the aspiration level. Our second set of suggestions is based on comparing our theory with theories that predict similar outcomes but make different assumptions. Research oriented to comparing the explanatory power of these different theories will help identify potential boundary conditions of the extended model proposed here.

7.1 Research on Mechanisms

Translating our theorized mechanisms into research is straightforward and offers the opportunity to make quick progress. A key step here is to examine whether ambiguity enables self-enhancement. This matters because both inside and outside the organization, formalization of the assessment criteria removes ambiguity and hence forces the decision-maker to respond to performance on a specific goal, whereas goal ambiguity allows detachment from a goal and possibly also reduces personal involvement. There is already research showing that ambiguous goals, aspiration levels, or feedback allow self-enhancement and hence inaction in the face of performance below aspiration levels on a specific goal (Audia et al., 2015; Joseph and Gaba, 2015; Smith and Chae, 2017). An obvious and important extension of this research is examination of organizations with complex goals such as hybrid organizations that pursue commercial and social goals (Battilana and Dorado, 2010; Boone and Özcan, 2016; Smith and Besharov, 2017). Much of the literature on hybrid organizations focuses on internal arrangements that enable organizations to pursue incompatible goals seen as having equal importance but is less concerned with whether and how decision-makers make changes in response to performance on these multiple goals. Interestingly, this literature highlights flexibility of interpretation and responses as a key feature of hybrid organizations. Flexibility of interpretation and responses is also a key feature in the extended model. There is, however, a difference in emphasis on the source of this flexibility. While we view flexibility as stemming from individual decision-makers' propensity to switch from a problem-solving orientation to a self-enhancing orientation, research on hybrid organizations gives greater importance to flexibility motivated by a commitment to preserve the hybrid identity of the organization. Analyses of how hybrid organizations respond to performance on multiple goals may allow additional testing of propositions advanced in this rich and growing literature while simultaneously exploring points of convergence and tension with the extended model of performance feedback.

Studies of hybrid organizations should only be considered a first step because multiple goals are central to many organizations and positions in organizations. An example of significant interest to scholars in organization theory is organizations with profitability and safety goals, such as organizations operating dangerous technologies (Baum and Dahlin, 2007; Gaba and Greve, 2019). The more general case is organizations that have profitability goals but also have brands built on costly activities such as maintenance of high quality. Consumer-facing organizations such as car makers (Haunschild and Rhee, 2004; Hu and Bettis, 2018), restaurants (Durand, Rao, and Monin, 2007), hotels (Wang, Wezel, and Forgues, 2016), food and beverage makers (Hsu, Roberts, and Swaminathan, 2012; Malter, 2014), and other makers of branded goods are in a continuous tug-of-war between the profitability goal and the costly but important quality goal. We should know more about the conditions that influence how decision-makers in these organizations respond to performance on multiple goals.

Research on ambiguous goals is often conducted at the organizational level of analysis because the goals are more clearly specified and behaviors are more observable at this level. This has led to a neglect of a larger phenomenon that concerns the behavior of more organizational participants: At any organizational level we find individuals filling roles that involve a mixture of goals. These goals may be specified clearly or not and may be incentivized or not, but they are usually well known to the individual. To the extent that they are formalized, the extended model predicts that a problem-solving orientation will follow. What is less frequently known is how decision-maker prioritizes multiple goals when the priority order is not formalized, leading to significant goal ambiguity.

Research on how individual organizational members react to performance feedback when there is goal ambiguity is especially urgent because the effects on employees can include decisions with dramatic consequences. We are writing this in the context of the COVID-19 pandemic after having read press reports that nearly all cardiopulmonary resuscitation (CPR) procedures to save advanced-stage patients have been unsuccessful and have probably been harmful to patients neglected as a result of the concentration of medical staff around each CPR event. The press also reports that very few advanced-age and prior-condition patients connected to a ventilator have survived, again to the detriment of others because ventilators have been scarce. Medical staff at all levels understand that saving the patient on their shift and in their room is important, but so is reducing the overall impact of an epidemic. How do these multiple goals with ambiguous trade-offs guide their decisions?

Fortunately, most organizational participants face less dramatic choices, but they still handle multiple goals with some ambiguity. Future research could draw on the extended model to tackle questions like the following: What is the effect of (1) the sheer number of goals the decision-maker is aware of, (2) the proximity of each goal to the decision-maker (e.g., ROA is an organizationally remote goal for most decision-makers), (3) the ambiguity in operationalizing and tracking performance within each goal, and (4) the ambiguity in preference ordering among the goals at any given time. These questions hark back to an old and neglected line of learning research on how choices are influenced by how goals are specified and measured (March, 1978). Economists have been attracted to the question of how incentives coupled to any given goal affect decisions (e.g., Gibbons, 1998), but progress on this single-goal question is limited unless these four fundamental questions on how goals interrelate are answered well. It is very rare that a decision-maker faces only one goal.

The degree of centralization of decisions that impact subunits is related to the abovementioned questions and introduces additional opportunities for future research. Our extended model proposes that, when centralization is greater and thus top managers participate in subunit decisions, a problem-solving orientation is more likely because top managers by virtue of their lesser involvement in subunit activities perceive low subunit performance as less threatening than subunit managers do. This draws on the idea that personal involvement is a key condition prompting self-enhancement. Centralization, however, may introduce other complications. First, centralization of decisions can detach the subunit manager from those decisions and lead to protective self-enhancing cognitions and behaviors – most obviously, by allocating responsibility for low performance to centralized decisions and claiming high performance along other goal dimensions related to actions still under the subunit manager's control. Second, centralization through incentive schemes prescribes actions indirectly, but still so clearly that the subunit manager may allocate responsibility for low performance to the incentive system rather than to own decisions, and so engage in self-enhancement. These are just two examples of the broader idea that self-enhancing responses can take a variety of forms even under conditions that our model expects to be conducive to a problem-solving orientation. For this reason, we view an examination of the different ways in which individuals in organizations self-enhance as an important research direction.

The link between personal involvement and the motivational orientation decision-makers adopt in response to performance on multiple goals raises important questions regarding firm governance mechanisms. An impression given by work on this topic (Westphal and Bednar, 2005; Tuggle, Schnatterly, and Johnson, 2010a; Tuggle et al., 2010b) is that an active board of directors compensates for the deficiencies of CEOs that are passive in the face of low organizational performance. Nonetheless, this interpretation overlooks a possible scenario raised by our theory: Active governance by the board may elevate personal involvement to the point where board members may feel as threatened by low performance as the top managers they are expected to control. If boards are more likely to engage in self-enhancement when things go wrong, who will then solve the problems evidenced by low performance? The dilemma is that a board should be sufficiently involved to deter management from self-enhancement behaviors, but not so involved that it also engages in self-enhancement. Governance research has not taken this scenario into account, and accordingly its recommendations may require additional scrutiny. We are noting this not to claim that CEOs should not be governed, but rather to make the point that under conditions of elevated involvement by the board such governance has a cost: biased assessments of performance arising from self-enhancement.

Formalization of performance assessment includes assignment of responsibility to the subunit manager both for actions taken and for performance on one or multiple goals, and this should lead to a stronger problem-solving orientation. Again, this is the theoretical expectation, and we currently do not have sufficient evidence to claim that it holds. We do have clear opportunities for research to examine the effects of formalization on firm and subunit behaviors, thanks to data that are available or easy to collect. For example, governance reform initiatives have led to boards adopting formal procedures for evaluating directors and board decision processes (Rowley, Shipilov, and Greve, 2017; Shipilov et al., 2019), and these are likely to be reflected in greater transparency to investors and closer examination of CEO decisions. Many environmental groups create formalized assessments and rankings of organizations, such as the J.D. Powers quality assessments of automobiles, the ISO 9000 process quality assessment (Terlaak and King, 2006), and the KLD rankings of corporate social responsibility (Chatterji, Levine, and Toffel, 2009). Other formalized assessment processes are generated through automatic customer feedback, such as those provided by online platforms (Wang et al., 2016; Greve and Song, 2017).

These assessments and rankings create three kinds of variation. The first is that many of them cover only some firms, either because they are voluntary (e.g., ISO 9000) or because they are done selectively (e.g., KLD). The second is that some assessments do not rank firms, whereas others do and hence are both a formalized assessment and potentially a goal (high rank) in themselves. The third is that numerical ratings or rankings can place firms high or low, and this can affect self-enhancement versus problem-solving just as powerfully as the formalization of a ranking (Rowley et al., 2017). Given the increased prevalence of ratings systems and their proven effects across industries (Elsbach and Kramer, 1996; Sauder, 2006; Sauder and Espeland, 2009), there is room for much more research on how they affect the self-enhancement versus problem-solving orientation in firms with performance below aspiration levels.

At the subunit level, researchers face the problem of many organizations not being sufficiently open about their formalized performance assessment to allow easy research access. Some of these issues can be resolved by modifying experiments on self-enhancing reactions to performance feedback (e.g., Audia and Brion, 2007; Jordan and Audia, 2012; Audia et al., 2015) to also include conditions with different forms and levels of formalized assessment. However, organizational research is also rich with empirical work made possible by firms giving access to their internal records (see Bidwell, 2011; Kleinbaum, 2012; Castilla, 2015), and such research should be pursued.

Research on the effects of multiple institutional logics is closely related to the work on goal ambiguity covered earlier because the mechanism is similar, with multiple institutional logics giving rise to goal ambiguity and often also to organizational forms that have hybrid features. These two research streams can learn from each other and will often unite in a single investigation. The research on multiple logics has a domain that is larger because even organizations that are designed to have a single goal can become embedded in environments with multiple logics, through no initiative of their own, and accordingly face the possibility of responding to prescriptions and goals that other actors hold for them (Greve and Teh, 2018).

We already have some knowledge on organizational responses to multiple external pressures through work done in related areas of research. Institutional logics research (Greenwood et al., 2011; Thornton, Ocasio, and Lounsbury, 2012) and social movement research (Davis et al., 2005; Briscoe and Gupta, 2016) are rich sources of ideas on how institutional environments seek to impose themselves on organizations. So far, they have not progressed in examining responses to performance feedback, however, because most work in these traditions sees these institutional pressures as main effects rather than as modifiers to how organizations respond to their most valued goals (such as profitability). The extended model of performance feedback complements that work because it outlines a more agentic view of how decision-makers respond not simply to performance feedback but also to cultural prescriptions of what is appropriate. Specifically, decision-makers with a self-enhancement orientation may "use" what macro theorists generally conceive as external constraints to form favorable interpretations of ambiguous information. Indeed, ironically, our extended model implies that attempts to make organizations do more for society through the increasing influence of multiple logics can provide decision-makers with opportunities to do less. This point of intersection between the theory of performance feedback and macro research on logics is so important that work on how goal proliferation affects responses to performance feedback is urgently needed.

The theoretical expectation is that managers facing complex institutional environments with multiple goals in addition to the usual firm goals have significant leeway in playing these goals against each other. For example, research has already found low-profitability firms deciding not to engage in governance reform because profitability improvement is urgently needed or perhaps because the governance reform is not a valued goal (Rowley et al., 2017). Facing the internal profitability goal and the external governance reform goal introduced sufficient goal ambiguity to let firms avoid problem-solving. Conversely, observing other organizations failing on environmental goals can trigger problemistic search in organizations that are not experiencing performance shortfall (e.g., Desai, 2014), suggesting that it is especially easy to trigger problemistic search when the organizational decision-makers have no reason to engage in self-enhancement.

Indeed, goal ambiguity can also originate from a mixture of internal goals that are difficult to reconcile or prioritize. Research on such mixtures of goals has just barely started, but has indicated that organizations are less responsive, suggesting that some degree of self-enhancement occurs (Hu and Bettis, 2018). Irreconcilable internal goals currently present an unsolved problem for the theory and evidence. If the theoretical reasoning and modest evidence from internal and external goal conflicts translates into conflicts among internal goals, the potential for decision-makers to exploit the resulting ambiguity to avoid problemistic search is high.

Research on the effects of power is important because power is the mechanism that can enable resistance against a problem-solving approach when the performance is below aspiration levels and either low centralization or high formalization prevents self-enhancing responses. To advance such research, researchers need to address the question of how to measure the power of organizational decision-makers. Fortunately progress has been made in measuring organizational power, much of it based on resource dependence theory (Pfeffer and Salancik, 1978; Wry, Cobb, and Aldrich, 2013), and these tools can be used along with advances from other research streams. Later work has added important details such as CEO cooptation of the board through selective recruitment of loyal board members (Westphal and Zajac, 1995). This work has shown that the type of boards with great CEO control – because directors are demographically similar to the CEO or have friendship ties to the CEO – result in less changes in response to low performance, consistent with CEO self-enhancement (Westphal and Bednar, 2005). Indeed, the work on CEO power relative to the board is quite rich in discovered mechanisms, including such subtle but effective mechanisms as control over the board agenda (Tuggle et al., 2010b; Joseph, Ocasio, and McDonnell, 2014), with greater agenda control allowing the CEO to respond less to performance below the aspiration level, as a self-enhancement orientation would predict.

7.2 Theoretical Comparisons

The extended model of performance feedback differs from analyses that take on a more stringent cognitive characterization of action (e.g., Ocasio, 1997). Theories that emphasize the cognitive component generally hold that beliefs guide action and that belief updating stems from unbiased assessment of evidence. Our extended model, by acknowledging the influence of personal involvement on motives, implies that, as Kunda (1987: 637) puts it, "the cognitive apparatus is harnessed in the service of motivational ends." Whereas individuals not personally involved in an activity display unbiased assessments of negative information and let their preexisting beliefs guide action, those who are personally involved alter their beliefs to reduce self-threat and let the changed beliefs guide action. Focusing on responsiveness to multiple goals, beliefs about which goals are most critical may change as a result of salient threats to the self-image. The contrast between these two approaches hinges on whether motivation can override pure cognitive effects, and experimental work manipulating these factors, similar to Smith and Chae (2017) and Audia et al. (2015), will help test the contingencies outlined in the extended model and identify boundary conditions.

The extended model also differs from analyses that view identity as a constraint on action. In those views, identity is a permanent filter on what actors see as relevant to define how to act. These views are related to the old insight that experience colors interpretation of events but take the further step of assuming a personally felt identity associated with experience, increasing the rigidity. We do not dispute that such effects are found. Our model implies, however, that actors may be willing to put their identity aside to give attention to features of the situation that help them form favorable evaluations of their self-image or gain rewards in the pursuit of goals. Motivation prevails over identity or at least prompts decision-makers to think of identity in more flexible terms. Again, personal involvement plays a critical role since it is the feature of our model that ties the tendency to protect one's self-image to self-enhancing assessments. When personal involvement is absent or weak, identity has a stronger impact on how the situation is assessed. Thus, in our model the identity effect is not "always on"; it is triggered by lack of personal involvement. For example, a CEO with a background in finance, who generally gives greater importance to financial metrics, may not let her finance identity inhibit the self-enhancing propensity to elevate in importance marketing goals that are producing better outcomes than financial goals. Identity-based theorizing assumes temporal consistency in preferences, whereas our extended model recognizes the likelihood of temporal inconsistency under conditions of high personal involvement. There is much research on how strong organizational identities shape behaviors, but these implications of our extended model have not been investigated.

At the individual, organizational, and environmental level, our extended model posits different mechanisms that alter the reaction to performance feedback, as one should expect given the difference of these levels of analysis. The alert reader will have noticed a common factor though: power. Taking an apparent problem seriously, searching for a solution, and enacting a solution that has been found are all influenced by power in our extended model. As our discussion showed, the expected effect is not necessarily that more power leads to more action. This is an important theoretical implication that needs empirical testing. More broadly, it fits a movement toward greater considerations of how power affects organizations (Wry et al., 2013). It still differs from the usual resource dependence predictions because, in the extended model, power counteracts factors that force decision-makers into problem-solving. Hence, power is unimportant if performance feedback indicates that there is no problem to solve. Also, it is less important if decision-maker self-enhancement is already enabled, as one would expect from, for example, a decision-maker handling ambiguous goal dimensions and lacking formalized performance assessment. The effects of power on decision-maker orientation are not needed to resist urgent calls for problem-solving because ambiguity and lack of formalization means that there are no such calls to begin with.

7.3 Conclusion

The core model of performance feedback is a fundamental model of organizational behavior. It proved to be broadly applicable, but also to be overly parsimonious, leading to the modified model. The modified model is also fundamental and broadly applicable, and for a wide range of phenomena it predicts and describes outcomes very well. Still, the need to explicitly incorporate multiple goals has led us to propose the extended model we describe here.

The addition of tensions between problemistic search and self-enhancement has not made the model any less fundamental, and we believe it has extended the range of phenomena it predicts and explains well. As a result, future research has two main tasks. The first is to test whether the model is correct as specified here. This section lists our suggestions on how to conduct such tests, but the model is so flexible and fundamental that many more are possible. The second is to explore its boundaries. What organizational behaviors can be understood using this model, as opposed to the simpler core or modified model? How might incorporation of the extended model improve other theories that are loosely built on the behavioral theory of the firm?

In the long run, the second of these questions might be the most important. After all, the behavioral theory of the firm in general, and especially problemistic search, is incorporated as an assumption in many organization theory models. The theory used to derive mimetic isomorphism rested on the behavioral theory of the firm (DiMaggio and Powell, 1983). Adaptive views of the organizational behaviors such as resource dependence rely on problem-solving reasoning (Pfeffer and Salancik, 1978). In the heyday of organizational ecology, problemistic search was often used as a micro-theory of organizational action (Barnett, Greve, and Park, 1994). Some papers on network and alliance theory assume that performance feedback guides establishment of interorganizational ties (Baum et al., 2005). What these treatments have in common is reliance on the core model rather than the more elaborate models that have been developed since. How will the theories change if they are integrated with performance feedback as currently modeled? Taking that step will allow theoretical and empirical advances with potential so high that we cannot assess it now.

8 Conclusion

The extended model of performance feedback should be placed into the greater context of how organizational theory has evolved so far and continues to evolve. Organizational theory started with the organization as the dominant level of analysis, as in the behavioral theory of the firm (Cyert and March, 1963), but soon added the environmental (macro) level of analysis as well as individual and group (micro) levels of analysis. It then separated, with much more active research streams at the micro and macro levels than at the organizational level of analysis. Research on performance feedback is centered on the organizational level of analysis and has revitalized this level, but it has also reached out to the more micro and macro levels of analyses. This is a recent development representative of current discontent with a divided organizational theory and indicative of a concern about the insights missed by such artificial divisions (e.g., Morgeson and Hofmann, 1999; Hitt et al., 2007).

Our extended model is part of a movement toward a modern synthesis of organization theory that seeks to establish stronger links among the main levels of analysis (Battilana and Dorado, 2010; Greenwood et al., 2011; Thornton, Ocasio, and Lounsbury, 2014). Specifically, problem discovery by internal decision-makers directs strategic change but problem discovery stems from performance assessments that reflect the influence of environmental and organizational conditions as well as decision-makers' individual characteristics. This modern synthesis seeks to capture key elements of a more complex world than many previous depictions, but it still draws much of its appeal from its familiarity with organizations that we observe and participate in. As the extended model demonstrates, it also draws its appeal from solving significant theoretical problems with an analytical framework that has few moving parts. How decision-makers respond to performance on multiple goals depends on whether they adopt a problem-solving or a self-enhancement orientation; the theory does not consider any third alternative. Factors at the individual-, organizational-, or environmental-level influence their response, but the effects are easy to specify and are so far few – only three – at each level of analysis. Even with this simple analytical framework, we were able to outline significant opportunities for future research.

The extended model, although simple, leaves significant room for empirical investigation and for adding new mechanisms from the data as well as from new theorizing. We expect most theory and evidence to center on the performance above and below aspiration levels, multiple goals, and problem-solving and self-enhancement. We also anticipate most research to focus on the three levels of analysis we have treated in this Element – individual, organization, and environment – though we recognize the importance of also considering the group level. There still is significant room to ask new questions because organizational goals have different sources and interrelations, aspiration levels are shaped by experiences, and the mechanisms we believe trigger either self-enhancement or problem-solving are likely to be incomplete. We stop our theoretical treatment here because we have covered the mechanisms we see as most promising for explaining organizational behaviors, but we do not claim that this is the end of the road. We expect the next book on this topic to contain insights that we have not foreseen or imagined.

References

Anand, B. N., K. F. Barnett, and E. L. Carpenter 2007 "Random House." Harvard Business School Publishing, Case no. 9–704–438.

Anand, B. N., M. G. Rukstad, and C. Kostring 2005 "Bertelsmann AG." Harvard Business School Publishing, Case no. 9–703–405.

Argote, L. and E. Miron-Spektor 2011 "Organizational learning: From experience to knowledge." Organization Science, 22: 1123–1137.

Audia, P. G. and S. Brion 2007 "Reluctant to change: Self-enhancing responses to diverging performance measures." Organizational Behavior & Human Decision Processes, 102: 255–269.

Audia, P. G., S. Brion, and H. R. Greve 2015 "Self-assessment, self-enhancement, and the choice of comparison organizations for evaluating organizational performance." Advances in Strategic Management: Cognition and Strategy, 35: 89–118.

Audia, P. G. and J. A. Goncalo 2007 "Past success and creativity over time: A study of inventors in the hard disk drive industry." Management Science, 53: 1–15.

Audia, P. G. and H. R. Greve 2006 "Less likely to fail? Low performance, firm size, and factory expansion in the shipbuilding industry." Management Science, 52: 83–94.

Audia, P. G., E. A. Locke, and K. G. Smith 2000 "The paradox of success: An archival and a laboratory study of strategic persistence following a radical environmental change." Academy of Management Journal, 43: 837–853.

Audia, P. G., H. E. Rousseau, and S. Brion 2021 "CEO power and nonconforming reference group selection." Organization Science, forthcoming.

Audia, P. G. and O. Sorenson 2001 "A multilevel analysis of organizational success and inertia." London School of Business: Manuscript.

Barnard, C. I. 1938 The Functions of the Executive. Cambridge, MA: Harvard University Press.

Barnett, W. P., H. R. Greve, and D. Y. Park 1994 "An evolutionary model of organizational performance." Strategic Management Journal, 15: 11–28.

Bartley, T. and C. Child 2011 "Movements, markets and fields: The effects of anti-sweatshop campaigns on U.S. firms, 1993–2000." Social Forces, 90: 425–451.

Battilana, J. and S. Dorado 2010 "Building sustainable hybrid organizations: The case of commercial microfinance organizations." Academy of Management Journal, 53: 1419–1440.

Baum, J. A. C. and K. B. Dahlin 2007 "Aspiration performance and railroads' patterns of learning from train wrecks and crashes." Organization Science, 18: 368–385.

Baum, J. A. C., T. J. Rowley, A. V. Shipilov, and Y.-T. Chuang 2005 "Dancing with strangers: Aspiration performance and the search for underwriting syndicate partners." Administrative Science Quarterly, 50: 536–575.

Benner, M. J. and M. Tripsas 2012 "The influence of prior industry affiliation on framing in nascent industries: the evolution of digital cameras." Strategic Management Journal, 33: 277–302.

Berg, J. M. 2016 "Balancing on the creative highwire: Forecasting the success of novel ideas in organizations." Administrative Science Quarterly, 61: 433–468.

Bidwell, M. 2011 "Paying more to get less: The effects of external hiring versus internal mobility." Administrative Science Quarterly, 56: 369–407.

Blagoeva, R. R., T. J. Mom, J. J. Jansen, and G. George 2020 "Problem-solving or self-enhancement? A power perspective on how CEOs affect R&D search in the face of inconsistent feedback." Academy of Management Journal, 63: 332–355.

Blau, P. M. 1955 The Dynamics of Bureaucracy. Chicago, IL: University of Chicago Press.

Blettner, D. P., Z.-L. He, S. Hu, and R. A. Bettis 2015 "Adaptive aspirations and performance heterogeneity: Attention allocation among multiple reference points." Strategic Management Journal, 36: 987–1005.

Boeker, W. 1989 "The development and institutionalization of subunit power in organizations." Administrative Science Quarterly, 34: 388–410.

Boone, C. and S. Özcan 2016 "Ideological purity vs. hybridization trade-off: When do Islamic banks hire managers from conventional banking?" Organization Science, 27: 1380–1396.

Briscoe, F., M. K. Chin, and D. C. Hambrick 2014 "CEO ideology as an element of the corporate opportunity structure for social activists." Academy of Management Journal, 57: 1786–1809.

Briscoe, F. and A. Gupta 2016 "Social activism in and around organizations." The Academy of Management Annals, 10: 671–727.

Bromiley, P. 1991 "Testing a causal model of corporate risk taking and performance." Academy of Management Journal, 34: 37–59.

Bromiley, P. and J. D. Harris 2014 "A comparison of alternative measures of organizational aspirations." Strategic Management Journal, 35: 338–357.

Bromley, P. and J. W. Meyer 2015 Hyper-organization: Global Organizational Expansion. Oxford University Press.

Burt, R. S., K. P. Christman, and H. C. Kilburn 1980 "Testing a structural theory of corporate cooptation: Interorganizational directorate ties as a strategy for avoiding market constraints on profits." American Sociological Review, 45: 821–841.

Campbell, W. K. and C. Sedikides 1999 "Self-threat magnifies the self-serving bias: A meta-analytic integration." Review of General Psychology, 3: 23–43.

Castilla, E. J. 2015 "Accounting for the gap: A firm study manipulating organizational accountability and transparency in pay decisions." Organization Science, 26: 311–333.

Chadwick, P. 1992 A Psychological Study of Paranoia and Delusional Thinking. New York: Routledge.

Chatterji, A. K., D. I. Levine, and M. W. Toffel 2009 "How well do social ratings actually measure corporate social responsibility?" Journal of Economics & Management Strategy, 18: 125–169.

Chatterji, A. K. and M. W. Toffel 2010 "How firms respond to being rated." Strategic Management Journal, 31: 917–945.

Christensen, C. M. and J. L. Bower 1996 "Customer power, strategic investment, and the failure of leading firms." Strategic Management Journal, 17: 197–218.

Cohen, M. D., J. G. March, and J. P. Olsen 1972 "A garbage can model of organizational choice." Administrative Science Quarterly, 17: 1–25.

Cyert, R. M. and J. G. March 1963 A Behavioral Theory of the Firm. Englewood Cliffs, NJ: Prentice-Hall.

Davis, G. F., D. McAdam, W. R. Scott, and M. N. Zald 2005 Social Movements and Organization Theory. Cambridge: Cambridge University Press.

Davis, G. F. and M. S. Mizruchi 1999 "The money center cannot hold: Commercial banks in the U. S. system of governance." Administrative Science Quarterly, 44: 215–239.

Delmas, M. A. and M. W. Toffel 2008 "Organizational responses to environmental demands: opening the black box." Strategic Management Journal, 29: 1027–1055.

Desai, V. M. 2008 "Constrained growth: How experience, legitimacy, and age influence risk taking in organizations." Organization Science, 19: 594–608.
2014 "The impact of media information on issue salience following other organizations' failures." Journal of Management, 40: 893–918.

DiMaggio, P. J. and W. W. Powell 1983 "The iron cage revisited: Institutional isomorphism and collective rationality in organizational fields." American Sociological Review, 48: 147–160.

Diwas, K. C., B. R. Staats, and F. Gino 2013 "Learning from my success and from others' failure: Evidence from minimally invasive cardiac surgery." Management Science, 59: 2435–2449.

Dunning, D., J. A. Meyerowitz, and A. D. Holzberg 1989 "Ambiguity and self-evaluation: The role of idiosyncratic trait definitions in self-serving assessments of ability." Journal of Personality and Social Psychology, 57: 1082.

Durand, R., H. Rao, and P. Monin 2007 "Code and conduct in French cuisine: Impact of code changes on external evaluations." Strategic Management Journal, 28: 455–472.

Edelman, L. B. 1992 "Legal ambiguity and symbolic structures: Organizational mediation of civil rights law." American Journal of Sociology, 97: 1531–1576.

Edwards, R. 1979 Contested Terrain: The Transformation of the Workplace in the Twentieth Century. New York: Basic Books.

Elsbach, K. D. and R. M. Kramer 1996 "Members' responses to organizational identity threats: Countering the business week rankings." Administrative Science Quarterly, 41: 442–476.

Elvira, M. M. and M. E. Graham 2002 "Not just a formality: Pay system formalization and sex-related earnings effects." Organization Science, 13: 601–617.

Felson, R. B. 1981 "Self-and reflected appraisal among football players: A test of the Meadian hypothesis." Social Psychology Quarterly, 44: 116–126.

Festinger, L. 1954 "A theory of social comparison processes." Human Relations, 7: 117–140.

Fiegenbaum, A. 1990 "Prospect theory and the risk-return association." Journal of Economic Behavior and Organization, 14: 184–203.

Fiegenbaum, A. and H. Thomas 1988 "Attitudes towards risk and the risk return paradox: Prospect theory explanations." Academy of Management Journal, 31: 395–407.

Friedland, R. and R. Alford 1991 "Bringing society back: Symbols, practices, and institutional contradictions." In W. W. Powell, and P. DiMaggio (eds.), The New Institutionalism in Organizational Analysis: 232–263. Chicago: Chicago University Press.

Gaba, V. and H. R. Greve 2019 "Safe or profitable? The pursuit of conflicting goals." Organization Science, 30: 647–667.

Gaba, V. and J. Joseph 2013 "Corporate structure and performance feedback: Aspirations and adaptation in m-form firms." Organization Science, 24: 1102–1119.

Gavetti, G., H. R. Greve, D. A. Levinthal, and W. Ocasio 2012 "The behavioral theory of the firm: Assessment and prospects." Academy of Management Annals, 6: 1–40.

Gibbons, R. 1998 "Incentives in organizations." Journal of Economic Perspectives, 12: 115–132.

Govindarajan, V. 1988 "A contingency approach to strategy implementation at the business-unit level: integrating administrative mechanisms with strategy." Academy of management Journal, 31: 828–853.

Greenwood, R., M. Raynard, F. Kodeih, E. R. Micelotta, and M. Lounsbury 2011 "Institutional complexity and organizational responses." Academy of Management Annals, 5: 317–371.

Greve, H. R. 1998 "Performance, aspirations, and risky organizational change." Administrative Science Quarterly, 44: 58–86.

2003a "A behavioral theory of R&D expenditures and innovation: Evidence from shipbuilding." Academy of Management Journal, 46: 685–702.

2003b "Investment and the behavioral theory of the firm: Evidence from shipbuilding." Industrial and Corporate Change, 12: 1051–1076.

2003c Organizational Learning from Performance Feedback: A Behavioral Perspective on Innovation and Change. Cambridge, UK: Cambridge University Press.

2008 "A behavioral theory of firm growth: Sequential attention to size and performance goals." Academy of Management Journal, 51: 476–494.

2011 "Positional rigidity: Low performance and resource acquisition in large and small firms." Strategic Management Journal, 32: 103–114.

Greve, H. R. and V. Gaba 2020 "Performance feedback in organizations and groups: common themes." In L. Argote, and J. Levine (eds.), Handbook of Group and Organizational Learning: 315–336. Oxford: Oxford University Press.

Greve, H. R. and S. Y. Song 2017 "Amazon warrior: How a platform can restructure industry power and ecology." Advances in Strategic Management, 37: 299–335.

Greve, H. R. and D. Teh 2018 "Goal selection internally and externally: A behavioral theory of institutionalization." International Journal of Management Reviews, 20: S19–S38.

Guinote, A. 2017 "How Power Affects People: Activating, wanting, and goal seeking." Annual Review of Psychology, 68: 353–381.

Gulati, R. and M. Gargiulo 1999 "Where do interorganizational networks come from?" American Journal of Sociology, 104: 1439–1493.

Haunschild, P. R. and M. Rhee 2004 "The role of volition in organizational learning: The case of automotive product recalls." Management Science, 50: 1545–1560.

Heilman, M. E., C. J. Block, and P. Stathatos 1997 "The affirmative action stigma of incompetence: Effects of performance information ambiguity." Academy of Management Journal, 40: 603–625.

Hillman, A. J. 2005 "Politicians on the board of directors: Do connections affect the bottom line?" Journal of Management, 31: 464–481.

Hillman, A. J., M. C. Withers, and B. J. Collins 2009 "Resource dependence theory: A review." Journal of Management, 35: 1404–1427.

Hinings, B. and R. E. Meyer 2018 Starting Points: Intellectual and Institutional Foundations of Organization Theory. Cambridge: Cambridge University Press.

Hitt, M. A., P. W. Beamish, S. E. Jackson, and J. E. Mathieu 2007 "Building theoretical and empirical bridges across levels: Multilevel research in management." Academy of Management Journal, 50: 1385–1399.

Hoffman, A. J. 1999 "Institutional evolution and change: Environmentalism and the U.S. chemical industry." Academy of Management Journal, 42: 351–371.

Hsu, G., P. W. Roberts, and A. Swaminathan 2012 "Evaluative schemas and the mediating role of critics." Organization Science, 23: 83–97.

Hu, S. and R. A. Bettis 2018 "Multiple organization goals with feedback from shared technological task environments." Organization Science, 29: 873–889.

Jordan, A. H. and P. G. Audia 2012 "Self-enhancement and learning from performance feedback." Academy of Management Review, 37: 211–231.

Joseph, J. and V. Gaba 2015 "The fog of feedback: Ambiguity and firm responses to multiple aspiration levels." Strategic Management Journal, 36: 1960–1978.

Joseph, J., R. Klingebiel, and A. J. Wilson 2016 "Organizational structure and performance feedback: Centralization, aspirations, and termination decisions." Organization Science, 27: 1065–1083.

Joseph, J., W. Ocasio, and M.-H. McDonnell 2014 "The structural elaboration of board independence: Executive power, institutional logics, and the adoption of CEO-only board structures in U.S. corporate governance." Academy of Management Journal, 57: 1834–1858.

Kacperczyk, A., C. M. Beckman, and T. P. Moliterno 2015 "Disentangling risk and change: Internal and external social comparison in the mutual fund industry." Administrative Science Quarterly, 60: 228–262.

Kahneman, D. and A. Tversky 1979 "Prospect theory: An analysis of decision under risk." Econometrica, 47: 263–291.

Kelly, K. J. 2003 "Godoff gone at Random." New York Post.

Keltner, D., D. H. Gruenfeld, and C. Anderson 2003 "Power, approach, and inhibition." Psychological Review, 110: 265–284.

Kirkpatrick, D. D. 2003 "Searching for motives in Random House ouster." New York Times.

Kleinbaum, A. M. 2012 "Organizational misfits and the origins of brokerage in intrafirm networks." Administrative Science Quarterly, 57: 407–452.

Kolker, R. 2001 "Waiting for Godoff." New York Magazine.

Kotiloglu, S., Y. Chen, and T. Lechler 2019 "Organizational Responses to Performance Feedback: A Meta-Analytic Review." Strategic Organization, forthcoming.

Kunda, Z. 1987 "Motivated inference: Self-serving generation and evaluation of causal theories." Journal of Personality and Social Psychology, 53: 636–647. 1990 "The case for motivated reasoning." Psychological Bulletin, 108: 480–498.

Lant, T. K. 1992 "Aspiration level adaptation: An empirical exploration." Management Science, 38: 623–644.

Lant, T. K., F. J. Milliken, and B. Batra 1992 "The role of managerial learning and interpretation in strategic persistence and reorientation: An empirical exploration." Strategic Management Journal, 13: 585–608.

Lehman, D. W., J. Hahn, R. Ramanujam, and B. J. Alge 2011 "The dynamics of the performance-risk relationship within a performance period: The moderating role of deadline proximity." Organization Science, 22: 1613–1630.

Levinthal, D. A. 1991 "Random walks and organizational mortality." Administrative Science Quarterly, 36: 397–420.

Levinthal, D. A. and J. G. March 1993 "The myopia of learning." Strategic Management Journal, 14: 95–112.

Levitt, B. and J. G. March 1988 "Organizational learning." In W. R. Scott, and J. Blake (eds.), Annual Review of Sociology, 14: 319–340. Palo Alto, CA: Annual Reviews.

Lopes, L. L. 1987 "Between hope and fear: The psychology of risk." Advances in Experimental Social Psychology, 20: 255–295.

Lounsbury, M. 2001 "Institutional sources of practice variation: Staffing college and university recycling programs." Administrative Science Quarterly, 46: 29–56.

Lucas, G. J., J. Knoben, and M. T. Meeus 2018 "Contradictory yet coherent? Inconsistency in performance feedback and R&D investment change." Journal of Management, 44: 658–681.

Malter, D. 2014 "On the causality and cause of returns to organizational status: Evidence from the Grands Crus Classés of the Médoc." Administrative Science Quarterly, 59: 271–300.

Manns, C. L. and J. G. March 1978 "Financial adversity, internal competition, and curriculum change in a university." Administrative Science Quarterly, 23: 541–552.

March, J. G. 1978 "Bounded rationality, ambiguity, and the engineering of choice." Bell Journal of Economics, 9: 587–608.

March, J. G. and Z. Shapira 1992 "Variable risk preferences and the focus of attention." Psychological Review, 99: 172–183.

March, J. G. and H. Simon 1958 Organizations. New York: Wiley.

Mautner, G. and M. Learmonth 2020 "From administrator to CEO: Exploring changing representations of hierarchy and prestige in a diachronic corpus of academic management writing." Discourse and Communication, 14: 273–293.

Mazmanian, M. and C. M. Beckman 2018 "'Making' your numbers: Engendering organizational control through a ritual of quantification." Organization Science, 29: 357–379.

Meyer, J. W. and B. Rowan 1977 "Institutionalized organizations: Formal structure as myth and ceremony." American Journal of Sociology, 83: 340–363.

Meyer, J. W., W. R. Scott, and D. Strang 1987 "Centralization, fragmentation, and school district complexity." Administrative Science Quarterly, 32: 186–201.

Mezias, S. J., Y. R. Chen, and P. R. Murphy 2002 "Aspiration-level adaptation in an American financial services organization: A field study." Management Science, 48: 1285–1300.

Miller, D. and M.-J. Chen 1994 "Sources and consequences of competitive inertia: A study of the U.S. airline industry." Administrative Science Quarterly, 39: 1–23.

Mintzberg, H. 1979 The Structuring of Organizations. Englewood Cliffs, NJ: Prentice-Hall.

Moliterno, T. P., N. Beck, C. M. Beckman, and M. Meyer 2014 "Knowing your place: Social performance feedback in good times and bad times." Organization Science, 25: 1684–1702.

Morgeson, F. P. and D. A. Hofmann 1999 "The structure and function of collective constructs: Implications for multilevel research and theory development." Academy of Management Review, 24: 249–265.

Ocasio, W. 1997 "Towards an attention-based theory of the firm." Strategic Management Journal, 18: 187–206.

Owen-Smith, J. and W. W. Powell 2001 "To patent or not: Faculty decisions and institutional success at technology transfer." The Journal of Technology Transfer, 26: 99–114.

Pache, A.-C. and F. Santos 2010 "When worlds collide: The internal dynamics of organizational responses to conflicting institutional demands." Academy of Management Review, 35: 455–476.

Park, S. H., J. D. Westphal, and I. Stern 2011 "Set up for a fall: The insidious effect of flattery and opinion conformity toward corporate leaders." Administrative Science Quarterly, 56: 257–302.

Pfeffer, J. 1981 Power in Organizations. Marshfield, MA: Pitman.

Pfeffer, J. and C. T. Fong 2005 "Building organization theory from first principles: The self-enhancement motive and understanding power and influence." Organization Science, 16: 372–388.

Pfeffer, J. and G. R. Salancik 1978 The External Control of Organizations. New York: Harper and Row.

Posen, H. E., T. Keil, S. Kim, and F. D. Meissner 2018 "Renewing research on problemistic search—A review and research agenda." Academy of Management Annals, 12: 208–251.

Purdy, J. M. and B. Gray 2009 "Conflicting logics, mechanisms of diffusion, and multilevel dynamics in emerging institutional fields." Academy of Management Journal, 52: 355–380.

Rowley, T. I., A. V. Shipilov, and H. R. Greve 2017 "Board reform versus profits: The effect of rankings on the adoption of governance practices." Strategic Management Journal, 38: 815–833.

Ruefli, T. W. 1990 "Mean-variance approaches to risk-return relationships in strategy: Paradox lost." Management Science, 36: 368–380.

Salancik, G. R. and J. Pfeffer 1974 "The bases and use of power in organizational decision making: The case of a university." Administrative Science Quarterly, 19: 453–473.

Sauder, M. 2006 "Third parties and status position: How the characteristics of status systems matter." Theory and Society, 35: 299–321.

Sauder, M. and W. N. Espeland 2009 "The discipline of rankings: Tight coupling and organizational change." American Sociological Review, 74: 63–82.

Scott, W. R. 1987 Organizations: Rational, Natural and Open Systems, 2nd ed. Englewood Cliffs, NJ: Prentice-Hall.

Sedikides, C. and M. J. Strube 1997 "Self evaluation: To thine own self be good, to thine own self be sure, to thine own self be true, and to thine own self be better." Advances in Experimental Social Psychology: 29: 209–269.

Sengul, M. and J. Gimeno 2013 "Constrained delegation: Limiting subsidiaries' decision rights and resources in firms that compete across multiple industries." Administrative Science Quarterly, 58: 420–471.

Sharkey, A. J. and P. Bromley 2015 "Can ratings have indirect effects? Evidence from the organizational response to peers' environmental ratings." American Sociological Review, 80: 63–91.

Shinkle, G. A. 2012 "Organizational aspirations, reference points, and goals." Journal of Management, 38: 415–455.

Shipilov, A. V., H. R. Greve, and T. J. Rowley 2019 "Is all publicity good publicity? The impact of direct and indirect media pressure on the adoption of governance practices." Strategic Management Journal, 40: 1368–1393.

Siggelkow, N. and D. A. Levinthal 2003 "Temporarily divide to conquer: Centralized, decentralized, and reintegrated organizational approaches to exploration and adaptation." Organization Science, 14: 650–669.

Simon, H. A. 1947 Administrative Behavior. New York: Macmillan.

Singh, J. V. 1986 "Performance, slack, and risk taking in organizational decision making." Academy of Management Journal, 29: 562–585.

Smith, E. B. and H. Chae 2017 "The effect of organizational atypicality on reference group selection and performance evaluation." Organization Science, 28: 1134–1149.

Smith, W. K. and M. L. Besharov 2019 "Bowing before dual gods: How structured flexibility sustains organizational hybridity." Administrative Science Quarterly, 64: 1–44.

Sosa, M. L. 2011 "From old competence destruction to new competence access: Evidence from the comparison of two discontinuities in anticancer drug discovery." Organization Science, 22: 1500–1516.

Staw, B. M. 1976 "Knee-deep in the big muddy: A study of escalating commitment to a chosen course of action." Organizational Behavior and Human Decision Processes, 16: 27–44.

Staw, B. M., S. G. Barsade, and K. W. Koput. 1997 "Escalating at the credit window: A longitudinal study of bank executives' recognition and write-off of problem loans." Journal of Applied Psychology, 82: 132–142.

Staw, B. M., L. E. Sandelands, and J. E. Dutton 1981 "Threat-rigidity effects in organizational behavior: A multi-level analysis." Administrative Science Quarterly, 26: 501–524.

Suddaby, R. and R. Greenwood 2005 "Rhetorical strategies of legitimacy." Administrative Science Quarterly, 50: 35–67.

Terlaak, A. and A. A. King 2006 "The effect of certification with the ISO 9000 quality management standard: A signaling approach." Journal of Economic Behavior & Organization, 60: 579–602.

Tetlock, P. E., L. Skitka, and R. Boettger 1989 "Social and cognitive strategies for copying with accountability: Conformity, complexity, and bolstering." Journal of Personality and Social Psychology, 57: 632–640.

Thornton, P. H. 2001 "Personal versus market logics of control: A historically contingent theory of the risk of acquisition." Organization Science, 12: 294–311.

2002 "The rise of the corporation in a craft industry: Conflict and conformity in institutional logics." Academy of Management Journal, 45: 81–101.

2004 Markets from Culture: Institutional Logics and Organizational Decisions in Higher Education Publishing. Stanford, California: Stanford Business Books.

Thornton, P. H. and W. Ocasio 1999 "Institutional logics and the historical contingency of power in organizations: Executive succession in the higher education publishing industry." American Journal of Sociology, 105: 801–843.

Thornton, P. H., W. Ocasio, and M. Lounsbury 2012 The Institutional Logics Perspective: A New Approach to Culture, Structure and Process. Oxford: Oxford University Press.

Tripsas, M. 2009 "Technology, identity, and inertia through the lens of 'the digital photography company'." Organization Science, 20: 441–460.

Tuggle, C. S., K. Schnatterly, and R. A. Johnson 2010a "Attention patterns in the boardroom: How board composition and processes affect discussion of entrepreneurial issues." Academy of Management Journal, 53: 550–571.

Tuggle, C. S., D. G. Sirmon, C. R. Reutzel, and L. Bierman 2010b "Commanding board of director attention: Investigating how organizational performance and CEO duality affect board members' attention to monitoring." Strategic Management Journal, 31: 946–968.

Tushman, M. L. and P. Anderson 1986 "Technological discontinuities and organizational environments." Administrative Science Quarterly, 31: 439–465.

Wang, T., F. C. Wezel, and B. Forgues 2016 "Protecting market identity: When and how do organizations respond to consumers' devaluations?" Academy of Management Journal, 59: 135–162.

Weber, M. 1978 Economy and Society. Berkeley, CA: University of California Press.

Westphal, J. D. and M. K. Bednar 2005 "Pluralistic ignorance in corporate boards and firms' strategic persistence in response to low firm performance." Administrative Science Quarterly, 50: 262–298.

Westphal, J. D. and E. J. Zajac 1995 "Who shall govern? CEO/board power, demographic similarity, and new director selection." Administrative Science Quarterly, 40: 60–83.

Wiseman, R. M. and P. Bromiley 1991 "Risk-return associations: Paradox or artifact? An empirically tested explanation." Strategic Management Journal, 12: 231–241.

Wry, T., J. A. Cobb, and H. E. Aldrich 2013 "More than a metaphor: Assessing the historical legacy of resource dependence and its contemporary promise as a theory of environmental complexity." Academy of Management Annals, 7: 441–488.

Zhang, C. M. and H. R. Greve 2018 "Delayed adoption of rules: A relational theory of firm exposure and state cooptation." Journal of Management, 44: 3336–3363.

Acknowledgments

We would like to thank the many people who made this book possible. First are the scholars whose work inspired the thinking behind our joint effort, particularly Ed Locke and Jim March. The influence of these foundational scholars on the perspective on multiple goals proposed here is deep and extends well beyond citing their work. As for the articles on performance feedback that have taken us to this particular point in our journey, we are greatly indebted to many very sophisticated coauthors and colleagues who have helped us develop our thinking by contributing ideas and advice. Finally, we owe a special thanks to Royston Greenwood and Nelson Phillips for their excellent editorial guidance.

Cambridge Elements ☰

Organization Theory

Nelson Phillips
Imperial College London

Nelson Phillips is the Abu Dhabi Chamber Professor of Strategy and Innovation at Imperial College London. His research interests include organization theory, technology strategy, innovation, and entrepreneurship, often studied from an institutional theory perspective.

Royston Greenwood
University of Alberta

Royston Greenwood is the Telus Professor of Strategic Management at the University of Alberta, a Visiting Professor at the University of Cambridge, and a Visiting Professor at the University of Edinburgh. His research interests include organizational change and professional misconduct.

About the Series

Organization theory covers many different approaches to understanding organizations. Its focus is on what constitutes the how and why of organizations and organizing, bringing understanding of organizations in a holistic way. The purpose of Elements in Organization Theory is to systematize and contribute to our understanding of organizations.

Cambridge Elements ≡

Organization Theory

Printed in the United States
By Bookmasters